Better Homes and Gardens®

chicken

familydinners

Better Homes and Gardens®

chicken

familydinners

JG
PRESS

This book is printed on acid-free paper.

Copyright © 2011 by Meredith Corporation, Des Moines, IA. All rights reserved.

Published by World Publications Group, Inc., 140 Laurel Street, East Bridgewater, MA 02333, www.wrldpub.com

Library of Congress Cataloging-in-Publication Data

Better homes and gardens chicken family dinners.
    p. cm.
  title: Chicken family dinners
  Includes index.
  ISBN 978-1-57215-690-6 (cloth); 978-1-57215-738-5 (cloth) -- ISBN 978-1-57215-691-3 (pbk.)
  1. Cooking (Chicken) 2. Cookbooks. I. Better homes and gardens. II. Title: Chicken family dinners.
  TX750.5.C45B4759 2010
  641.6'65--dc22

                                      2010042343

Printed in China

10 9 8 7 6 5 4 3 2 1

Better Homes and Gardens

Test Kitchen

Our seal assures you that every recipe in *Chicken Family Dinners* has been tested in the Better Homes and Gardens Test Kitchen®. This means that each recipe is practical and reliable and meets our high standards of taste appeal. We guarantee your satisfaction with this book for as long as you own it.

contents

soups, stews AND CHILIES

Cheesy Chicken Tortellini Soup, *recipe page 9*

parmesan-pesto CHICKEN SOUP

A delicious slice of Parmesan and pesto toast tops each bowl of this easy-to-make chicken soup.

Start to Finish: 35 minutes
Makes: 4 main-dish servings

- 2 **14-ounce cans chicken broth**
- 1 **teaspoon dried Italian seasoning, crushed**
- 2 **cloves garlic, minced**
- 12 **ounces skinless, boneless chicken breast halves, cut into bite-size pieces**
- ¾ **cup small shell macaroni**
- 2 **½-inch-thick slices Italian bread, halved crosswise**
- 2 **tablespoons purchased basil pesto**
- ¼ **cup finely shredded Parmesan cheese (1 ounce)**
- ¾ **cup loose-pack frozen peas**
- ¼ **cup thinly sliced green onions**

1 In a medium saucepan combine chicken broth, Italian seasoning, and garlic; bring to boiling.

2 Add chicken and uncooked macaroni to broth. Return mixture to boiling; reduce heat. Simmer, uncovered, for 8 to 9 minutes or until pasta is tender and chicken is no longer pink, stirring occasionally.

3 Meanwhile, preheat broiler. Spread one side of each halved bread slice with pesto. Sprinkle with Parmesan cheese. Place bread on broiler rack. Broil 3 to 4 inches from heat about 2 minutes or just until cheese begins to melt.

4 Add peas and green onions to broth mixture; cook for 2 minutes more. Top individual servings with the cheesy toasted bread.

Nutrition Facts per serving: 330 cal., 9 g total fat (1 g sat. fat), 56 mg chol., 1103 mg sodium, 31 g carbo., 29 g pro.

cheesy chicken TORTELLINI SOUP

This soup is no ordinary chicken soup. Chunks of chicken and vegetables share the bowl with lightly cooked leafy greens and plump, cheesy tortellini.

Start to Finish: 40 minutes
Makes: 6 (1⅓-cup) servings

- 12 ounces skinless, boneless chicken breast halves
- 2 teaspoons olive oil
- 3 cloves garlic, minced
- 2 14.5-ounce cans reduced-sodium chicken broth
- 3 cups sliced fresh mushrooms
- 1¾ cups water
- 2 medium carrots, cut into matchstick strips (1 cup)
- 2 cups packed torn fresh purple kale or spinach
- 1 teaspoon dried tarragon, crushed
- 1 9-ounce package refrigerated cheese-filled tortellini

1 Rinse chicken; pat dry. Cut the chicken into ¾-inch pieces. In a Dutch oven heat olive oil over medium-high heat. Cook and stir chicken and garlic in hot oil for 5 to 6 minutes or until chicken is no longer pink. Stir in chicken broth, mushrooms, water, carrots, kale (if using), and tarragon.

2 Bring mixture to boiling; reduce heat. Simmer, covered, for 2 minutes. Add tortellini. Simmer, covered, for 5 to 6 minutes more or until tortellini is tender. Stir in the spinach (if using).

Nutrition Facts per serving: 254 cal., 7 g total fat (2 g sat. fat), 50 mg chol., 596 mg sodium, 27 g carbo., 21 g pro.

chicken MINESTRONE SOUP

Start to Finish: 45 minutes
Makes: 8 (about 1⅓-cup)
servings

1 tablespoon olive oil

1 cup sliced carrots

½ cup chopped celery

½ cup chopped onion

3 14-ounce cans reduced-sodium chicken broth

2 15-ounce cans cannellini beans (white kidney beans), rinsed and drained

8 ounces skinless, boneless chicken breast, cut into bite-size pieces

1 cup fresh green beans cut into ½-inch pieces (4 ounces)

¼ teaspoon black pepper

1 cup dried bow tie pasta

1 medium zucchini, quartered lengthwise and cut into ½-inch-thick slices

1 14.5-ounce can diced tomatoes with basil, garlic, and oregano, undrained

1 In a 5- to 6-quart Dutch oven heat oil over medium heat. Add carrots, celery, and onion; cook for 5 minutes, stirring frequently. Add chicken broth, cannellini beans, chicken, green beans, and pepper. Bring to boiling; add uncooked pasta. Reduce heat. Simmer, uncovered, for 5 minutes.

2 Stir in zucchini. Return to boiling; reduce heat. Simmer, uncovered, for 8 to 10 minutes more or until pasta is tender and green beans are crisp-tender. Stir in undrained tomatoes; heat through.

Nutrition Facts per serving: 173 cal., 3 g total fat (0 g sat. fat), 16 mg chol., 818 mg sodium, 27 g carbo., 17 g pro.

wild rice CHICKEN SOUP

Garlic and a splash of Madeira give this chicken and rice soup high-intensity flavor. It's a sunny twist on old-fashioned chicken and rice soup.

Start to Finish: 25 minutes
Makes: 6 servings

- 1 6.2-ounce package quick-cooking long grain and wild rice mix
- 2 14.5-ounce cans reduced-sodium chicken broth
- 1 tablespoon snipped fresh thyme or 1 teaspoon dried thyme, crushed
- 4 cloves garlic, minced
- 4 cups chopped tomatoes
- 1 9-ounce package frozen chopped cooked chicken breast
- 1 cup finely chopped zucchini
- ¼ teaspoon freshly ground black pepper
- 1 tablespoon Madeira or dry sherry (optional)

1 Prepare rice mix according to package directions, except omit the seasoning packet and the margarine.

2 Meanwhile, in a Dutch oven combine the chicken broth, dried thyme (if using), and garlic. Bring to boiling. Stir in the tomatoes, chicken, zucchini, pepper, and if using, fresh thyme.

3 Return to boiling; reduce heat. Simmer, covered, for 5 minutes. Stir in cooked rice and if desired, Madeira. Heat through.

Nutrition Facts per serving: 236 cal., 5 g total fat (1 g sat. fat), 38 mg chol., 440 mg sodium, 31 g carbo., 18 g pro.

creamy BROCCOLI-CHICKEN SOUP

This incredibly creamy soup is packed with vegetables, poultry, and just the right amount of seasoning.

Start to Finish: 25 minutes
Makes: 4 servings

1½ cups small broccoli florets

 1 cup sliced fresh mushrooms

 ½ cup shredded carrot

 ¼ cup chopped onion

 ¼ cup butter

 ¼ cup all-purpose flour

1½ teaspoons snipped fresh basil
      or ½ teaspoon dried basil,
      crushed

 ¼ teaspoon black pepper

 3 cups milk

 1 cup half-and-half or light
      cream

 1 tablespoon white wine
      Worcestershire sauce

 2 teaspoons instant chicken
      bouillon granules

1½ cups chopped cooked chicken
      or turkey

      Coarse ground black pepper

1 In a large saucepan cook and stir broccoli, mushrooms, carrot, and onion in butter over medium heat for 6 to 8 minutes or until vegetables are tender.

2 Stir in flour, basil, and the ¼ teaspoon pepper. Add milk, half-and-half, Worcestershire sauce, and bouillon granules. Cook and stir until thickened and bubbly. Stir in chicken; heat through. Ladle soup into bowls, sprinkle with coarse ground pepper.

Nutrition Facts per serving: 435 cal., 27 g total fat (15 g sat. fat), 116 mg chol., 764 mg sodium, 23 g carbo., 26 g pro.

hot and sour CHICKEN SOUP

A satisfying soup doesn't have to take long to make. This Chinese-style favorite takes less than 15 minutes to cook.

Makes: 4 servings

- 2 **teaspoons peanut oil or cooking oil**
- 4 **ounces sliced fresh shiitake mushrooms**
- 2 **cloves garlic, minced**
- 2 **14.5-ounce cans reduced-sodium chicken broth**
- 2 **tablespoons white vinegar or rice vinegar**
- 2 **tablespoons reduced-sodium soy sauce**
- ½ **teaspoon crushed red pepper or 1 teaspoon chili oil**
- 2 **cups packaged shredded cabbage with carrot (cole-slaw mix) or shredded Chinese cabbage**
- 1 **cup shredded cooked chicken**
- 2 **tablespoons water**
- 1 **tablespoon cornstarch**
- 1 **teaspoon toasted sesame oil**

1 In a large saucepan heat oil over medium heat. Add mushrooms and garlic. Cook for 4 minutes, stirring occasionally. Stir in broth, vinegar, soy sauce, and red pepper; bring to boiling. Stir in coleslaw mix or cabbage and cooked chicken; reduce heat. Simmer, uncovered, for 5 minutes.

2 Combine water and cornstarch, stirring until smooth; stir into soup. Bring to boiling. Cook about 2 minutes or until slightly thickened. Remove saucepan from heat; stir in sesame oil.

Nutrition Facts per serving: 157 cal., 7 g total fat (1 g sat. fat), 34 mg chol., 889 mg sodium, 9 g carbo., 15 g pro.

chicken and potato CHOWDER

A south-of-the-border flavor dominates this thick, savory chowder. Green chile peppers provide a kick, and cilantro, a prominent herb in Mexican foods, adds the air of authenticity.

Start to Finish: 40 minutes
Makes: 4 servings

½ **cup chopped onion**

1 **tablespoon butter**

2 **cups fresh or frozen whole kernel corn**

1½ **cups reduced-sodium chicken broth**

1½ **cups chopped, peeled potato**

1 **4-ounce can diced green chile peppers, drained**

¼ **teaspoon coarsely ground black pepper**

2 **cups milk**

2 **tablespoons all-purpose flour**

5 **ounces cooked chicken, cut into thin strips (1 cup)**

2 **tablespoons snipped fresh cilantro or 2 teaspoons snipped fresh oregano**

1 In a large saucepan cook onion in hot butter for 3 to 4 minutes or until tender. Add corn, chicken broth, potato, chile peppers, and black pepper. Bring to boiling; reduce heat. Cover and simmer about 15 minutes or until potatoes are tender, stirring occasionally.

2 In a screw-top jar combine milk and flour; cover and shake well. Add to potato mixture. Cook and stir until thickened and bubbly. Add chicken and cilantro. Heat through.

Nutrition Facts per serving: 311 cal., 9 g total fat (4 g sat. fat), 49 mg chol., 446 mg sodium, 40 g carbo., 20 g pro.

buffalo CHICKEN SOUP

Start to Finish: 40 minutes
Makes: 6 servings

- 1 2¼- to 2½-pound deli-roasted chicken
- 2 tablespoons butter
- ½ cup coarsely chopped celery (1 stalk)
- ½ cup chopped onion (1 medium)
- 2 14-ounce cans reduced-sodium chicken broth
- 1½ cups milk
- 1 teaspoon bottled hot pepper sauce
- 1½ cups shredded mozzarella cheese (6 ounces)
- 1¼ cups crumbled blue cheese (5 ounces)
- ½ cup shredded Parmesan cheese (2 ounces)
- ⅓ cup all-purpose flour
   Bottled hot pepper sauce (optional)

1 Remove skin from chicken. Remove meat from bones; discard skin and bones. Coarsely shred meat; set aside. In 4-quart Dutch oven melt butter over medium heat. Add celery and onion; cook and stir until onion is tender. Stir in broth, milk, and the 1 teaspoon hot pepper sauce.

2 In a medium bowl toss together mozzarella, 1 cup of the blue cheese, the Parmesan cheese, and flour. Add gradually to soup, stirring after each addition just until melted. Stir in three-fourths of the shredded chicken; heat through. Top with remaining chicken and remaining ¼ cup blue cheese. If desired, pass additional hot sauce.

Nutrition Facts per serving: 490 cal., 28 g total fat (15 g sat. fat), 144 mg chol., 1,134 mg sodium, 12 g carbo., 45 g pro.

sage chicken DUMPLING SOUP

Prep: 35 minutes
Cook: 10 minutes
Makes: 8 servings

1 2- to 2½-pound deli-roasted
chicken

1 tablespoon olive oil

2 cups sliced fresh mushrooms

1 cup chopped onions
(2 medium)

¼ cup all-purpose flour

6 cups reduced-sodium chicken
broth

2 cups frozen peas

½ cup pitted kalamata olives,
halved

1 tablespoon lemon juice

1 teaspoon ground sage

Buttermilk Dumplings*

Thinly sliced green onions
(optional)

Fried Sage Sprigs** (optional)

① Remove and discard skin and bones from chicken. Cut chicken into chunks. Set aside. In a 4-quart Dutch oven heat oil over medium heat. Add mushrooms and onion; cook for 6 to 8 minutes or until mushrooms are tender and liquid has evaporated.

② Stir in flour until combined. Add broth all at once. Cook and stir until thickened and bubbly. Stir in chicken, peas, olives, lemon juice, and ground sage. Return to boiling.

③ Using two spoons, drop Buttermilk Dumplings dough into 8 mounds onto hot soup. Cover and simmer about 10 minutes or until a toothpick inserted in a dumpling comes out clean. (Do not lift cover during cooking.)

④ If desired, sprinkle each serving with green onions and top with Fried Sage Sprigs.

*Buttermilk Dumplings: In a medium bowl stir together 2 cups all-purpose flour, ½ teaspoon baking powder, ¼ teaspoon baking soda, and ¼ teaspoon salt. Stir in ¼ cup sliced green onions and 1 tablespoon snipped fresh flat-leaf parsley. Add 1 cup buttermilk and 2 tablespoons olive oil or vegetable oil. Stir just until moistened.

**Fried Sage Sprigs: In a medium saucepan heat ¼ cup olive oil over medium heat until hot but not smoky. Add 8 small fresh sage sprigs, two at a time; cook for 30 to 60 seconds or until crisp. Remove with slotted spoon and drain on paper toweling.

Nutrition Facts per serving: 367 cal., 12 g total fat (2 g sat. fat), 56 mg chol., 776 mg sodium, 37 g carbo., 25 g pro.

mexican chicken SOUP

Prep: 30 minutes
Bake: 20 minutes
Cook: 1 hour
Stand: 15 minutes
Oven: 425°F
Makes: 6 servings

2 to 2½ pounds meaty chicken
pieces (breast halves,
thighs, and drumsticks),
skin removed

6 cups water

2 cups coarsely chopped onion
(2 large)

2 cups coarsely chopped celery
(4 stalks)

1 cup coarsely chopped tomato
(1 large)

½ cup snipped fresh cilantro

1½ teaspoons salt

1 teaspoon ground cumin

¼ to ½ teaspoon cayenne
pepper

¼ to ½ teaspoon black pepper

1½ cups chopped carrots
(3 medium)

1 or 2 fresh poblano chile
peppers*

Sliced avocado (optional)

Fresh cilantro sprigs
(optional)

1 In a 4½-quart Dutch oven, combine chicken pieces, the water, 1 cup of the onion, 1 cup of the celery, the tomato, the snipped cilantro, salt, cumin, cayenne pepper, and black pepper. Bring to boiling; reduce heat. Cover and simmer for 40 to 50 minutes or until chicken is tender. Remove chicken pieces and set aside to cool slightly. Strain the broth mixture, reserving broth and discarding the vegetables.

2 Return the broth to the Dutch oven. Add the remaining 1 cup onion, the remaining 1 cup celery, and the carrots. Bring to boiling; reduce heat. Cover and simmer for about 20 minutes or until vegetables are tender.

3 Meanwhile, preheat oven to 425°F. Line a baking sheet with foil; set aside. Cut chile peppers in half lengthwise and remove seeds, stems, and veins.* Place pepper halves, cut sides down, on prepared baking sheet. Bake for 20 to 25 minutes or until skins are blistered and dark. Wrap peppers in the foil; let stand about 15 minutes or until cool enough to handle. Use a sharp knife to loosen the edges of the skins from the pepper halves; gently and slowly pull off the skin in strips. Discard skin. Chop peppers.

4 Remove chicken from bones; discard bones. Chop the chicken. Stir chicken and poblano peppers into broth mixture. Heat through. If desired, garnish with avocado slices and cilantro sprigs.

Nutrition Facts per serving: 158 cal., 5 g total fat (1 g sat. fat), 61 mg chol., 638 mg sodium, 7 g carbo., 21 g pro.

*Test Kitchen Tip: Because chile peppers contain volatile oils that can burn your skin and eyes, avoid direct contact with them as much as possible. When working with chile peppers, wear plastic or rubber gloves. If your bare hands do touch the peppers, wash your hands and nails well with soap and warm water.

french CHICKEN STEW

Prep: 30 minutes
Cook: 6 to 7 hours (low) or
3 to 4 hours (high)
Makes: 8 servings

4   cups sliced fresh button and/or
    stemmed shiitake mushrooms

1   14.5-ounce can diced
    tomatoes, undrained

1   cup diagonally sliced carrots
    (2 medium)

1   cup 1-inch pieces round red-
    skin potato (1 medium)

1   cup chicken broth

½   cup chopped onion (1 medium)

½   cup 1-inch pieces fresh green
    beans

½   cup pitted ripe olives, halved

½   cup dry white wine or
    chicken broth

2   tablespoons quick-cooking
    tapioca

1   teaspoon herbes de Provence
    or dried Italian seasoning,
    crushed

¾   teaspoon dried thyme, crushed

¼   teaspoon coarsely ground
    black pepper

8   skinless, boneless chicken
    thighs (1¾ to 2 pounds total)

½   teaspoon seasoned salt

1   14-ounce jar tomato pasta
    sauce or one 16-ounce jar
    Alfredo pasta sauce

    French bread (optional)

1 In a 5- to 6-quart slow cooker, combine mushrooms, undrained tomatoes, carrots, potato, broth, onion, green beans, olives, wine, tapioca, herbes de Provence, thyme, and pepper. Place chicken on top; sprinkle with seasoned salt.

2 Cover and cook on low-heat setting for 6 to 7 hours or on high-heat setting for 3 to 4 hours.

3 Stir in pasta sauce. If desired, serve with French bread.

Nutrition Facts per serving: 219 cal., 5 g total fat (1 g sat. fat), 83 mg chol., 629 mg sodium, 17 g carbo., 23 g pro.

chicken AND BLACK BEAN STEW

The whole family will love this chunky stew with chicken and turkey sausage. A touch of fiery chipotle in adobo (smoked jalapeño chiles canned in tomato sauce) provides the right amount of heat.

Prep: 20 minutes
Cook: 1 hour 20 minutes
Stand: 8 hours
Makes: 6 servings

- 2 cups dry black beans, rinsed
- 4 medium boneless, skinless chicken thighs, trimmed and cut into ½-inch chunks
- ¾ teaspoon salt, divided
- 3 links Italian turkey sausage, cut in half
- 1½ cups chopped onions
- 1 medium green bell pepper, chopped
- 1 tablespoon chopped garlic
- 1 teaspoon ground cumin
- 2 cans (14 ounces each) chicken broth
- 1 bay leaf
- 1 can (15 ounces) stewed tomatoes
- 1 tablespoon chopped chipotle chile in adobo*
- 3 tablespoons chopped fresh cilantro
- 1 container (8 ounces) fat-free plain yogurt

1 Soak beans according to package directions. Drain.

2 Sprinkle chicken with ¼ teaspoon of the salt. Heat large Dutch oven over medium-high heat 1 minute. Add chicken and sausage and cook 7 to 8 minutes or until browned, turning occasionally. Transfer to bowl; cover and refrigerate.

3 Reduce heat to medium. Add onions, bell pepper and garlic to Dutch oven and cook about 4 minutes or until vegetables are tender. Stir in cumin; cook 1 minute. Stir in broth, bay leaf, and beans; bring to boil. Reduce heat; simmer, covered, 50 to 55 minutes. Stir in chicken, sausage, tomatoes, chipotle, and remaining ½ teaspoon salt; cook 30 to 60 minutes more or until beans are tender. Ladle stew into four serving bowls. Top with cilantro and serve with yogurt.

Nutrition Facts per serving: 400 cal., 6.5 g total fat (1.5 g sat. fat), 52 mg chol., 1,333 mg sodium, 54 g carbo., 32 g pro.

*Note: Chipotle chiles in adobo are available in many supermarkets and at Mexican food stores.

chicken, barley, AND LEEK STEW

Leeks and carrots add fresh-from-the-garden appeal to chewy barley and tender chicken in this satisfying stew.

Prep: 20 minutes
Cook: 4 to 5 hours (low) or
          2 to 2½ hours (high)
Makes: 6 main-dish servings

1 **tablespoon olive oil**

1 **pound skinless, boneless chicken thighs, cut into 1-inch pieces**

1 **49-ounce can chicken broth**

1 **cup regular barley (not quick-cooking)**

3 **medium leeks, halved lengthwise and sliced**

2 **medium carrots, thinly sliced**

1½ **teaspoons dried basil or Italian seasoning, crushed**

¼ **teaspoon cracked black pepper**

   Salt

   Cracked black pepper

   Slivered fresh basil or snipped fresh parsley (optional)

1 In a large skillet heat olive oil over medium-high heat. Cook chicken in hot oil until browned, turning to brown evenly. In a 4- to 5-quart slow cooker combine chicken, chicken broth, barley, leeks, carrots, basil, and the ¼ teaspoon cracked black pepper.

2 Cover and cook on low-heat setting for 4 to 5 hours or on high-heat setting for 2 to 2½ hours or until barley is tender. Season to taste with salt and additional cracked black pepper. If desired, garnish with basil or parsley.

Nutrition Facts per serving: 253 cal., 7 g total fat (1 g sat. fat), 63 mg chol., 1,027 mg sodium, 27 g carbo., 21 g pro.

wild rice AND CHICKEN STEW

Cream of chicken soup, cooked chicken, and chicken broth triple the chicken flavor of this no-fuss meal in a bowl.

Prep: 15 minutes
Cook: 6 to 8 hours (low) or
        3 to 4 hours (high)
Makes: 8 to 10 servings

2½ **cups chopped cooked chicken (about 12 ounces)**

2 **cups sliced fresh mushrooms**

1 **cup coarsely shredded carrots (2 medium)**

1 **cup sliced celery (2 stalks)**

1 **10.5-ounce can condensed cream of chicken or cream of mushroom soup**

1 **6-ounce package long grain and wild rice mix**

5 **cups chicken broth**

5 **cups water**

1 In a 5- to 6-quart slow cooker combine chicken, mushrooms, carrots, celery, soup, uncooked rice mix, and the contents of the rice seasoning packet. Gradually stir in broth and the water.

2 Cover and cook on low-heat setting for 6 to 8 hours or on high-heat setting for 3 to 4 hours.

Nutrition Facts per serving: 221 cal., 7 g total fat (2 g sat. fat), 44 mg chol., 1,251 mg sodium, 23 g carbo., 18 g pro.

chicken-wild rice CHILI

Wild rice adds extra heartiness to this white-style chili.

Prep: 20 minutes
Cook: 35 minutes
Makes: 6 to 8 servings

- 1 **pound skinless, boneless chicken breast or turkey, cut into ½-inch pieces**
- 1 **tablespoon cooking oil**
- ¼ **cup chopped onion**
- ½ **teaspoon bottled minced garlic**
- 3 **cups water**
- 1 **14-ounce can chicken broth**
- ⅔ **cup wild rice, rinsed and drained**
- 2 **4-ounce cans diced green chile peppers**
- 2 **teaspoons chili powder**
- 1 **teaspoon ground cumin**
- 1 **15.25-ounce can whole kernel corn, drained**
- 1 **15- to 16-ounce can Great Northern beans, rinsed and drained**

  Bottled hot pepper sauce

  Shredded Monterey Jack cheese or Monterey Jack cheese with jalapeño peppers, shredded (optional)

  Dairy sour cream (optional)

  Snipped fresh parsley (optional)

1 In a 4- to 5-quart Dutch oven, cook chicken, half at a time, in hot oil until brown, adding onion and garlic with the last half of the chicken.

2 Stir in the water, broth, wild rice, undrained chile peppers, chili powder, and cumin. Bring to boiling; reduce heat. Simmer, covered, for 35 to 40 minutes or until wild rice is tender. Stir in corn and beans. Heat through. Season to taste with several dashes of bottled hot pepper sauce.

3 To serve, ladle into soup bowls. Serve with cheese and sour cream. If desired, garnish with parsley.

Nutrition Facts per serving: 324 cal., 5 g total fat (1 g sat. fat), 45 mg chol., 638 mg sodium, 43 g carbo., 28 g pro.

southwestern WHITE CHILI

When winter's wind chills your spirit, it's time for a bowl of this hearty south-of-the-border-style soup.

Prep: 20 minutes
Cook: 7 to 8 hours (low) or
3½ to 4 hours (high)
Makes: 8 servings

1 **cup chopped onion (1 large)**

4 **cloves garlic, minced**

2 **teaspoons ground cumin**

1 **teaspoon dried oregano, crushed**

¼ **teaspoon cayenne pepper**

3 **15.5-ounce cans Great Northern beans, rinsed and drained**

2 **4-ounce cans diced green chile peppers, undrained**

4 **cups chicken broth or reduced-sodium chicken broth**

3 **cups chopped cooked chicken (about 1 pound)**

2 **cups shredded Monterey Jack cheese (8 ounces)**

Dairy sour cream (optional)

Cilantro leaves (optional)

1 In a 3½- to 6-quart slow cooker place onion, garlic, cumin, oregano, cayenne pepper, beans, undrained chile peppers, broth, and cooked chicken. Stir to combine.

2 Cover and cook on low-heat setting for 7 to 8 hours or on high-heat setting for 3½ to 4 hours. Stir in the cheese until melted.

3 Ladle the chili into bowls. If desired, top servings with sour cream and cilantro.

Nutrition Facts per serving: 431 cal., 14 g total fat (7 g sat. fat), 72 mg chol., 671 mg sodium, 39 g carbo., 38 g pro.

chicken salsa CHILI

Prep: 15 minutes
Cook: 20 minutes
Makes: 6 servings

1 16-ounce jar thick-and-chunky
   salsa

1 15-ounce can yellow
   hominy or garbanzo beans
   (chickpeas), rinsed and
   drained

1 15-ounce can dark red kidney
   beans or black beans, rinsed
   and drained

1 14-ounce can chicken broth

1 9-ounce package frozen diced
   cooked chicken

1 4-ounce can diced green chile
   peppers, undrained

1 tablespoon chili powder

2 teaspoons bottled minced
   garlic (4 cloves) or
   ½ teaspoon garlic powder

¼ to ½ teaspoon crushed red
   pepper

¼ cup snipped fresh cilantro

2 tablespoons lime juice

   Chopped red onion and/or
   sliced green onion (optional)

   Shredded sharp cheddar
   cheese (optional)

   Chopped avocado (optional)

   Sour cream or plain low-fat
   yogurt (optional)

1 In a 4-quart Dutch oven combine salsa, hominy, beans, broth, chicken, undrained chile peppers, chili powder, garlic, and crushed red pepper. Bring to boiling; reduce heat. Cover and simmer for 20 minutes.

2 Just before serving, stir in cilantro and lime juice. If desired, top each serving with red onion, cheese, avocado, and/or sour cream.

Nutrition Facts per serving: 190 cal., 2 g total fat (0 g sat. fat), 23 mg chol., 1,200 mg sodium, 27 g carbo., 17 g pro.

white bean-CHICKEN CHILI

This Southwest-style white bean-and-chicken chili is studded with puffy, chewy hominy—corn that's been dried and then rehydrated. Either white or yellow hominy works equally well.

Start to Finish: 20 minutes
Makes: 4 servings

1 **tablespoon vegetable oil**

½ **cup chopped onion
(1 medium)**

1 **15- to 16-ounce can hominy,
drained**

1 **15- to 16-ounce can Great
Northern beans, rinsed and
drained**

1 **14-ounce can reduced-sodium
chicken broth**

1 **9-ounce package frozen
cooked chicken breast strips**

¼ **cup lime juice**

2 **tablespoons snipped fresh
cilantro leaves**

¼ **teaspoon ground cumin**

¼ **teaspoon black pepper**

½ **cup shredded Colby and
Monterey Jack cheese, or
cheddar cheese (2 ounces)**

Bottled green salsa

White corn tortilla chips

**Fresh cilantro leaves
(optional)**

1 In a large saucepan heat oil over medium heat. Add onion; cook and stir for 3 minutes. Stir in hominy, beans, broth, frozen chicken, lime juice, snipped cilantro, cumin, and pepper. Cover and bring to boiling over high heat, stirring occasionally.

2 Top each serving with cheese, salsa, and tortilla chips. If desired, garnish with cilantro leaves.

Nutrition Facts per serving: 434 cal., 14 g total fat (5 g sat. fat), 58 mg chol., 1,001 mg sodium, 48 g carbo., 31 g pro.

salads

Cool-as-a-Cucumber Chicken Salad, *recipe page 49*

fried CHICKEN SALAD

Peanut-coated chicken, orange sections, and fresh mozzarella top the mixed salad greens drizzled with a balsamic vinaigrette.

Prep: 35 minutes
Cook: 10 minutes
Makes: 6 main-dish servings

½ cup finely chopped peanuts

3 tablespoons fine dry bread crumbs

1 tablespoon snipped fresh basil

¼ to ½ teaspoon crushed red pepper

4 medium skinless, boneless chicken breast halves (about 1 pound total)

2 tablespoons margarine or butter, melted

2 tablespoons cooking oil

8 cups torn mixed greens

3 medium oranges, peeled and sectioned

3 medium tomatoes, cored and cut into wedges

8 ounces fresh mozzarella cheese, cut into ¼-inch-thick slices and quartered

3 tablespoons olive oil

3 tablespoons balsamic vinegar

1 tablespoon snipped fresh basil

¼ teaspoon salt

¼ teaspoon crushed red pepper

¼ teaspoon freshly ground pepper

1 For coating mixture, in a shallow dish combine peanuts, bread crumbs, 1 tablespoon basil, and ¼ teaspoon crushed red pepper. Set aside. Rinse chicken; pat dry. Brush each breast half with margarine. Dip in peanut mixture, pressing firmly to coat.

2 In a large skillet cook the chicken breasts in hot oil over medium-low heat for 10 to 12 minutes or until an instant-read thermometer inserted near the center registers 170°F, turning once. Cool slightly. Cut into ½-inch-thick slices.

3 Meanwhile, in a very large bowl combine greens, orange sections, tomato wedges, and cheese. In a screw-top jar combine olive oil, balsamic vinegar, 1 tablespoon snipped fresh basil, salt, ¼ teaspoon crushed red pepper, and freshly ground black pepper. Cover and shake well. Drizzle vinaigrette over all; toss to coat. Spoon salad onto large platter. Top with sliced chicken. Serve immediately.

Nutrition Facts per serving: 437 cal., 30 g total fat (8 g sat. fat), 61 mg chol., 384 mg sodium, 15 g carbo., 29 g pro.

cabbage-chicken TOSS

A food processor makes quick work of shredding the cabbages for this tasty main-dish salad.

Start to Finish: 30 minutes
Makes: 6 servings

4 medium skinless boneless chicken breast halves (1 pound total)

1 tablespoon cooking oil

4 cups shredded green cabbage

4 cups shredded red cabbage

4 cups shredded Napa cabbage

1 tablespoon finely shredded lemon peel

1 teaspoon salt

¾ teaspoon pepper

1 Cut chicken into thin bite-size strips. Heat oil in a wok or large skillet over medium-high heat. Add half of the chicken to the hot wok. Stir-fry for 2 to 3 minutes or until no pink remains. Remove from wok. Repeat with remaining chicken. (Add more oil as necessary during cooking.) Cool chicken slightly.

2 Combine chicken, cabbages, lemon peel, salt, and pepper in a very large bowl. Gently toss to mix well.

Nutrition Facts per serving: 138 cal., 4 g total fat (0 g sat. fat), 40 mg chol., 412 mg sodium, 8 g carbo., 16 g pro.

Make Ahead: Refrigerate, covered, up to 2 days.

oriental CHICKEN SALAD

The dressing softens the uncooked noodles to make fake croutons.

Prep: 30 minutes
Broil: 10 minutes
Makes: 4 servings

Pineapple-Sesame Dressing*

4 cups torn mixed greens (such as spinach, romaine, Chinese cabbage, and/or leaf lettuce)

2 cups fresh vegetables (such as bean sprouts; pea pods, halved crosswise; and/or cucumber strips)

1 cup coarsely chopped red cabbage

2 green onions, thinly sliced

1 3-ounce package Oriental-flavor ramen noodles (do not need seasoning packet)

4 small skinless, boneless chicken breast halves (¾ pound total)

   Nonstick spray coating

3 tablespoons reduced-sodium soy sauce

2 teaspoons grated fresh ginger

2 teaspoons sesame seeds

   Chive blossom flowers (optional)

1 Prepare Pineapple-Sesame Dressing; cover and chill until needed. In a large bowl toss together the mixed greens, desired fresh vegetables, red cabbage, and green onions. Break uncooked ramen noodles into small pieces; add to salad.

2 To prepare chicken, rinse chicken breasts; pat dry. Halve chicken breasts lengthwise. Spray the unheated rack of a broiler pan with nonstick coating. Place chicken breast halves on broiler rack. Stir together soy sauce and ginger; brush onto chicken. Broil 4 inches from heat for 10 to 12 minutes or until no pink remains, turning once and brushing with soy mixture. Remove chicken from heat; cool slightly.

3 Cut chicken into bite-size strips; add to vegetable mixture. Shake dressing and pour over the salad; toss to coat. Sprinkle sesame seeds over all. Garnish with chive blossom flowers, if desired. Serve immediately.

***Pineapple-Sesame Dressing:** In a screw-top jar combine ⅓ cup unsweetened pineapple juice, ¼ cup rice vinegar or white vinegar, 1 tablespoon water, 1 tablespoon reduced-sodium soy sauce, 2 teaspoons sugar, 1½ teaspoons toasted sesame oil, and ¼ teaspoon pepper. Cover and shake dressing mixture well.

Nutrition Facts per serving: 205 cal., 6 g total fat (1 g sat. fat), 48 mg chol., 677 mg sodium, 17 g carbo., 22 g pro.

poached chicken SALAD STACKUP

Start to Finish: 30 minutes
Makes: 4 servings

1 **lemon**
1 **pound skinless, boneless chicken breast halves, cut in 2-inch pieces**
1 **cup chicken broth**
1 **teaspoon dry oregano**
4 **cloves garlic, minced**
1 **seedless cucumber**
1 **5-ounce container Greek-style honey-flavored yogurt**
4 **tomatoes, sliced**
Salt and ground black pepper
Fresh oregano (optional)

❶ Finely shred peel from lemon; juice lemon. In saucepan combine peel, juice, chicken, broth, garlic and 1 teaspoon dried oregano; bring simmer over medium-high heat. Reduce heat and simmer, covered, 10 minutes or until no pink remains in chicken. Drain, reserving ⅓ cup cooking liquid.

❷ Meanwhile, chop half the cucumber; slice remaining. For dressing, place reserved cooking liquid in bowl; whisk in yogurt. Remove half the dressing and set aside. Add chicken to bowl along with chopped cucumber; toss to coat.

❸ Layer tomato and cucumber slices on plates. Top with chicken mixture. Drizzle with some of the reserved dressing. Season with salt and pepper. Top with fresh oregano, if desired. Pass remaining dressing.

Nutrition Facts per serving: 196 cal., 3 g total fat (1 g sat. fat), 68 mg chol., 480 mg sodium, 13 g carbo., 32 g pro.

thai chicken AND NECTARINE SALAD

A peppery-sweet dressing provides the crowning touch to this pasta salad entrée. Simply add warmed crusty French rolls.

Start to Finish: 40 minutes
Makes: 4 servings

- ¼ cup reduced-sodium chicken broth
- 3 tablespoons reduced-sodium soy sauce
- 2 tablespoons bottled hoisin sauce
- 1 tablespoon sugar
- 1 tablespoon salad oil or olive oil
- 2 teaspoons toasted sesame oil
- 3 cloves garlic, minced
- 1½ teaspoons grated fresh ginger
- 1 teaspoon crushed red pepper
- ⅛ teaspoon ground black pepper
- ¾ pound skinless, boneless chicken breast halves
- 4 ounces dried angel hair pasta
- 3 medium nectarines, plums, or peeled peaches, pitted and sliced
- 2 cups shredded bok choy
- 2 green onions, thinly sliced

1 For dressing, in a screw-top jar combine broth, soy sauce, hoisin sauce, sugar, salad or olive oil, sesame oil, garlic, ginger, crushed red pepper, and black pepper. Cover; shake well. Set aside.

2 In a covered large skillet cook chicken in a small amount of boiling water for 12 to 15 minutes or until tender and no longer pink; drain. Cool slightly; cut into cubes. Cook pasta according to package directions; drain.

3 In a large bowl toss pasta with 3 tablespoons of the dressing. Divide pasta mixture among four dinner plates. Top with the chicken, fruit, bok choy, and green onions. Drizzle with remaining dressing.

Nutrition Facts per serving: 359 cal., 9 g total fat (2 g sat. fat), 45 mg chol., 644 mg sodium, 46 g carbo., 23 g pro.

pulled CHICKEN SALAD

Store watercress, stems down, in ½ inch of clean water. Loosely cover and refrigerate for up to one week.

Makes: 4 servings

- 2 tablespoons frozen orange-tangerine or orange juice concentrate
- 1 tablespoon water
- 2 teaspoons toasted sesame oil
- ¼ teaspoon salt
- ⅛ teaspoon coarsely ground black pepper
- 12 ounce skinless, boneless chicken breast halves
- 3 cups watercress sprigs
- ¼ cup cocktail peanuts

1. In a small bowl combine juice concentrate, the water, sesame oil, salt, and pepper. Reserve 1 tablespoon of the juice mixture for brushing on chicken. Set aside remaining mixture for dressing.

2. Place steamer basket in a large skillet. Add water to skillet to just below bottom of basket. Bring to boiling. Place chicken in single layer in steamer basket; brush chicken with reserved 1 tablespoon juice mixture. Reduce heat to medium-low. Cover and steam for 10 to 12 minutes or until chicken is no longer pink (170°F).

3. Transfer chicken to cutting board; cool slightly. Using two forks, pull chicken apart into shreds.

4. To serve, in large salad bowl combine chicken, watercress, and peanuts. Add reserved dressing; toss gently to coat.

Nutrition Facts per serving: 186 cal., 8 g total fat (1 g sat. fat), 49 mg chol., 241 mg sodium, 5 g carbo., 23 g pro.

mango CHICKEN SALAD

This main-dish orange-draped salad makes a spectacular showing on a buffet table.

Start to Finish: 35 minutes
Makes: 6 servings

- 2 ripe mangoes, seeded, peeled, and coarsely chopped (2 cups)
- 1/3 cup extra virgin olive oil
- 2 tablespoons sherry vinegar or red wine vinegar
- 1/2 teaspoon sugar
- 4 medium skinless, boneless chicken breast halves
- 8 cups torn mixed salad greens
- 1/2 cup coarsely chopped pecans, walnuts, or almonds or 1/4 cup pine nuts, toasted
- 3 green onions, cut diagonally into 1/2-inch pieces
- 3 slices bacon, crisp-cooked, drained, and crumbled
- 1/4 cup extra virgin olive oil
- 1 tablespoon sherry vinegar or red wine vinegar
- 1/2 teaspoon sea salt or kosher salt
- 1/4 teaspoon freshly ground black pepper

1. For mango vinaigrette, in a food processor or blender combine chopped mangoes, the 1/3 cup oil, the 2 tablespoons sherry vinegar, and sugar. Cover; process or blend until mixture is smooth. Cover and chill in the refrigerator while preparing salad.

2. Place the chicken on the unheated rack of a broiler pan. Broil 5 to 6 inches from the heat for 12 to 15 minutes or until chicken is tender and no longer pink and an instant-read thermometer inserted into the chicken registers 170°F, turning once. (Or grill chicken on the rack of an uncovered grill directly over medium coals for 12 to 15 minutes or until chicken is tender and no longer pink and an instant-read thermometer inserted in the chicken registers 170°F, turning once halfway through grilling.)

3. Meanwhile, in a large bowl combine salad greens, nuts, onions, and bacon. Toss gently to mix. In a small bowl combine the 1/4 cup oil, the 1 tablespoon sherry vinegar, salt, and pepper. Drizzle over salad mixture. Toss gently to mix. Arrange on a large serving platter.

4. Cut chicken into bite-size strips. Arrange chicken on top of the greens mixture. Stir chilled mango vinaigrette; spoon over chicken. Serve immediately.

Nutrition Facts per serving: 419 cal., 30 g total fat (4 g sat. fat), 57 mg chol., 244 mg sodium, 14 g carbo., 25 g pro.

chicken WITH GREENS AND BRIE

Prep: 30 minutes
Cook: 12 minutes
Makes: 2 servings

- 3 cups torn mixed salad greens
- 1 cup seedless green grapes
- ½ cup walnut or pecan halves, toasted
- ¼ cup olive oil
- 2 tablespoons cider vinegar, white vinegar, or rice vinegar
- 1 tablespoon strawberry spreadable fruit
- ¼ cup refrigerated basil pesto
- ¼ cup chopped walnuts or pecans, toasted
- 2 skinless, boneless chicken breast halves (8 ounces total)
- 1 tablespoon olive oil
- 1 cup Marsala, cream sherry, or chicken broth
- 2 1- to 2-ounces wedges Brie
- 2 slices crusty country bread

1 For salad, in a large bowl combine greens, grapes, and nut halves; set aside. For dressing, in a small bowl whisk together ¼ cup oil, vinegar, and spreadable fruit; set aside. For pesto, in a small bowl combine pesto and chopped nuts; set aside.

2 In a large skillet heat oil over medium-high heat. Add chicken; cook about 3 minutes on each side or until brown. Remove skillet from heat; drain fat. Carefully add Marsala. Return skillet to heat. Bring to boiling; reduce heat. Simmer, uncovered, for 5 to 10 minutes or until chicken is no longer pink, turning chicken once. Remove chicken from skillet; discard Marsala.

3 Toss together salad and dressing. Transfer to dinner plates. Arrange chicken and Brie on top of greens. Spoon pesto mixture over chicken. Serve with bread.

Nutrition Facts per serving: 1,218 cal., 94 g total fat (13 g sat. fat), 98 mg chol., 654 mg sodium, 48 g carbo., 46 g pro.

wilted chicken salad WITH
POMEGRANATE DRESSING

Start to Finish: 30 minutes
Makes: 4 servings

¾ **cup pomegranate juice**

1 **14- to 16-ounce pkg. chicken tenderloins**

2 **tablespoons olive oil**

½ **medium red onion, cut lengthwise into thin wedges**

1 **tablespoon snipped fresh oregano or ½ teaspoon dried oregano, crushed**

¾ **teaspoon coarsely ground black pepper**

½ **teaspoon salt**

2 **tablespoons red wine vinegar**

2 **6-ounce pkg. baby spinach leaves**

½ **cup pomegranate seeds**

¼ **cup slivered almonds, toasted***

1 In a small saucepan bring pomegranate juice to boiling; boil gently, uncovered, 5 to 8 minutes or until reduced to ¼ cup. Remove from heat; set aside. Meanwhile, in a 12-inch skillet cook chicken in 1 tablespoon hot olive oil over medium-high heat for 6 to 8 minutes or until chicken is no longer pink, turning occasionally. Remove chicken from skillet. Keep warm.

2 Add onions, remaining oil, dried oregano (if using), pepper, and salt to skillet; cook for 3 to 5 minutes or until onion is just tender, stirring occasionally. Stir in reduced pomegranate juice and vinegar; bring to boiling. Boil 1 minute. Remove from heat and stir in fresh oregano (if using). Gradually add spinach, tossing just until spinach is wilted and combined.

3 Serve in large shallow dish. Top with chicken, pomegranate seeds, and nuts. Serve immediately.

Nutrition Facts per serving: 292 cal., 11 g total fat (2 g sat. fat), 58 mg chol., 425 mg sodium, 21 g carbo., 27 g pro.

***Test Kitchen Tip:** To toast nuts, spread the slivered almonds in a single layer in a shallow baking pan. Bake in a 350°F oven for 5 to 10 minutes or until light golden brown, watching carefully and stirring once or twice so the nuts don't burn. You can toast the nuts up to a day ahead, if desired.

cool-as-a-cucumber CHICKEN SALAD

Arrange chicken, melon, cucumber, and zucchini on greens and drizzle with refreshing lime and mint dressing.

Start to Finish: 25 minutes
Makes: 4 main-dish servings

- 2 **cups cubed cantaloupe and/or honeydew melon**
- 1 **cup finely chopped cucumber**
- 1 **cup finely chopped zucchini**
- ¼ **cup thinly sliced green onions**
- ⅓ **cup lime juice**
- 2 **tablespoons salad oil**
- 2 **tablespoons water**
- 2 **tablespoons snipped fresh cilantro or mint**
- 1 **tablespoon sugar**
- ⅛ **teaspoon ground white pepper**
- 4 **cups shredded leaf lettuce**
- 2 **cups shredded cooked chicken (10 ounces)**

1. In a large bowl toss together cantaloupe, cucumber, zucchini, and green onions.

2. For dressing, in a screw-top jar combine lime juice, oil, water, cilantro, sugar, and white pepper. Cover and shake well. Drizzle ½ cup of the dressing over the melon mixture. Toss lightly to coat.

3. Divide shredded lettuce among four dinner plates. Top with the melon mixture. Arrange chicken around edges of plates. Drizzle remaining dressing over chicken.

Nutrition Facts per serving: 258 cal., 12 g total fat (3 g sat. fat), 62 mg chol., 77 mg sodium, 16 g carbo., 22 g pro.

chicken-zucchini SALAD

When the vegetables abound in your garden or the farmers market pick out the season's best. Toss them with chicken in a dill- and citrus-scented mayonnaise for a refreshing summer salad.

Prep: 25 minutes
Chill: 4 hours
Makes: 6 to 8 servings

3 **cups shredded cooked chicken**

1 **medium zucchini or yellow summer squash, chopped (1¼ cups)**

1 **small fennel or kohlrabi bulb, trimmed and chopped (1¼ cups)**

4 **medium green onions, sliced**

1 **stalk celery, chopped**

1 **medium carrot, chopped**

2 **tablespoons snipped dried apricots (optional)**

Herbed Mustard Mayonnaise*

Torn salad greens

Salt and ground black pepper

1 In a large bowl combine chicken, zucchini, fennel, green onions, celery, carrot, and if desired, dried apricots. Pour Herbed Mustard Mayonnaise over chicken mixture; toss gently to coat. Cover and refrigerate for 4 to 24 hours.

2 To serve, line six to eight salad plates with salad greens. Stir chicken mixture; season to taste with salt and black pepper. Spoon the chicken mixture over salad greens.

***Herbed Mustard Mayonnaise:** In a small bowl combine ⅔ cup fat-free or light mayonnaise dressing, 4 teaspoons Dijon-style mustard, 1 tablespoon snipped fresh dill or tarragon, 1 teaspoon finely shredded lemon peel, 1 tablespoon lemon juice, 1 tablespoon frozen orange juice concentrate, and ¼ teaspoon black pepper. Makes about ¾ cup.

Nutrition Facts per serving: 193 cal., 6 g total fat (2 g sat. fat), 68 mg chol., 514 mg sodium, 11 g carbo., 23 g pro.

guacamole CHICKEN SALAD

Skim milk and buttermilk help to cut back on the fat in this creamy dressing.

Prep: 20 minutes
Cook: 10 minutes
Oven: 350°F
Makes: 4 servings

- 4 **small corn tortillas**
- 1 **medium-size avocado, peeled and pitted**
- 2 **tablespoons lime juice**
- ½ **cup skim milk**
- ⅓ **cup buttermilk**
- 2 **tablespoons chopped fresh cilantro**
- 2 **tablespoons chopped green onion**
- ¾ **tablespoon salt**
- 5 **drops hot-pepper sauce**
- 2 **cups shredded iceberg lettuce**
- 2 **cups shredded cooked chicken breast**
- 1 **large sweet red pepper, cut into strips**
- 1 **jar (6.3 ounces) baby corn, drained**

  Avocado slices (optional)

1 Preheat oven to 350°F.

2 Wrap tortillas in foil. Heat in 350°F oven for 10 minutes.

3 Puree avocado and lime juice in food processor. With motor running, add skim milk and buttermilk.*

4 Transfer mixture to small bowl. Stir in cilantro, onion, salt, and hot pepper sauce. Cover surface directly with plastic wrap. Refrigerate until serving.

5 Place equal amounts of lettuce, chicken, red pepper and corn on each warmed tortilla. Top with guacamole dressing. Garnish with avocado slice, if desired. Serve immediately.

Nutrition Facts per serving: 301 cal., 11 g total fat (2 g sat. fat), 50 mg chol., 668 mg sodium, 30 g carbo., 24 g pro.

*Note: For thinner dressing, add more skim milk, 1 tablespoon at a time.

strawberry spinach salad
WITH HICKORY-SMOKED CHICKEN

The hint of the grill comes from the smoked chicken in this main-dish salad.

Start to Finish: 45 minutes
Makes: 4 to 6 main-dish salads

Orange-Balsamic Vinaigrette*

1   6-ounce pkg. fresh baby spinach or 8 cups fresh baby or torn spinach and/or assorted torn greens

2   cups quartered or sliced strawberries and/or whole blueberries

8   ounces hickory-smoked cooked chicken or turkey, cut into bite-size pieces or 1½ cups chopped cooked chicken or turkey

4   ounces Gruyere, Swiss, Gouda, smoked cheddar, and/or Edam cheese, cut into bite-size strips

1   cup fresh enoki mushrooms and/or sliced fresh button mushrooms

½   cup loosely packed fresh Italian parsley leaves, snipped (¼ cup)

Freshly ground black pepper

1 Prepare Orange-Balsamic Vinaigrette. Cover and store in refrigerator while preparing the salad.

2 For salad, place spinach on a large serving platter or divide among individual dinner plates. Arrange strawberries, chicken, cheese, and mushrooms on spinach. Top with parsley.

3 Shake vinaigrette; pour over salad. Top with pepper.

*Orange-Balsamic Vinaigrette: In a screw-top jar combine ⅓ cup olive oil or vegetable oil; ¼ cup white balsamic vinegar, white wine vinegar, or cider vinegar; 1 teaspoon finely shredded orange peel; ¼ cup orange juice; 1 tablespoon snipped fresh Italian (flat-leaf) parsley; and ⅛ teaspoon salt. Cover and shake well to mix. Serve immediately or cover and store in refrigerator for up to 1 week. Makes about ¾ cup.

Nutrition Facts per serving: 413 cal., 29 g total fat (8 g sat. fat), 56 mg chol., 810 mg sodium, 19 g carbo., 22 g pro.

24-hour CHICKEN FIESTA SALAD

Chilling the salad for up to 24 hours allows the flavors to blend. Layer the ingredients one evening and have a ready-to-serve meal the next.

Prep: 30 minutes
Chill: 4 to 24 hours
Makes: 4 main-dish servings

- **4 cups torn iceberg, Boston, or Bibb lettuce**
- **½ cup shredded Monterey Jack cheese with jalapeño peppers (2 ounces)**
- **1 8-ounce can red kidney beans, rinsed and drained, or ½ of a 15-ounce can garbanzo beans, rinsed and drained (1 cup)**
- **1½ cups chopped cooked chicken or turkey (about 8 ounces)**
- **2 small tomatoes, cut into thin wedges**
- **½ of a small jicama (about 4 ounces), cut into bite-size strips (1 cup), or 1 cup shredded carrot**
- **½ cup sliced pitted ripe olives (optional)**
- **Chile Dressing***
- **¾ cup crushed tortilla chips (optional)**

1 Place the lettuce in a large (2-quart) salad bowl. Layer ingredients in the following order: cheese, beans, chicken, tomatoes, jicama, and, if desired, olives. Spread Chile Dressing evenly over salad, sealing to edge of bowl. Cover salad tightly with plastic wrap. Chill for 4 to 24 hours. To serve, toss lightly to coat evenly. If desired, sprinkle with crushed tortilla chips.

*Chile Dressing: In a small bowl stir together ½ cup mayonnaise or salad dressing, one 4-ounce can chopped canned green chile peppers, 1¼ teaspoons chili powder, and 1 clove garlic, minced. Makes about ¾ cup.

Nutrition Facts per serving: 444 cal., 32 g total fat (7 g sat. fat), 73 mg chol., 460 mg sodium, 17 g carbo., 26 g pro.

caesar salad WITH CHICKEN CROUTONS

All you need to do is bake prepared chicken nuggets (the "croutons" of this dish) to easily and quickly transform a classic Caesar salad into a satisfying main dish.

Prep: 15 minutes
Bake: 15 minutes
Makes: 4 servings

- **1 package (9 to 12 ounces) cooked, breaded, boneless chicken-breast nuggets**
- **1 medium head romaine lettuce (1 pound), torn into bite-size pieces**
- **1 medium head radicchio (½ pound), torn into bite-size pieces**
- **1 medium yellow pepper, finely chopped**
- **1 hard-cooked egg, finely chopped**
- **½ cup mayonnaise or salad dressing**
- **¼ cup freshly grated Parmesan cheese**
- **2 flat anchovy fillets**
- **2 tablespoons fresh lemon juice**
- **1 tablespoon water**
- **1 large clove garlic, crushed**
- **¼ teaspoon freshly ground pepper**
- **¼ cup freshly grated Parmesan cheese**

1 Cut each chicken-breast nugget into quarters. Arrange pieces on a large jelly-roll pan and bake according to package directions.

2 Meanwhile, toss romaine, radicchio, pepper, and egg in bowl. Set aside.

3 For the dressing, combine mayonnaise, ¼ cup Parmesan cheese, anchovy fillets, lemon juice, water, garlic, and ground pepper in a blender. Cover and blend until smooth. Pour dressing over salad and toss well. Add hot chicken and toss again. Serve immediately with ¼ cup Parmesan cheese.

Nutrition Facts per serving: 505 cal., 39 g total fat (9 g sat. fat), 107 mg chol., 909 mg sodium, 20 g carbo., 12 g pro.

ginger-lime CHICKEN SALAD

Lime juice, fresh ginger, and pumpkin seeds update chicken salad with a breezy tropical flavor. To keep your kitchen cool and save time, start with a purchased roasted chicken.

Start to Finish: 20 minutes
Makes: 2 servings

¼ **cup light mayonnaise dressing or salad dressing**
1 **tablespoon chopped red onion**
1 **tablespoon lime juice**
1 **teaspoon grated fresh ginger**
1 **small clove garlic, quartered**
1½ **cups roasted chicken breast cut into bite-size strips**
1 **stalk celery, cut lengthwise into thin ribbons**
1 **tablespoon salted pumpkin seeds or chopped peanuts**
Lime wedges (optional)

1 For dressing, in a blender container combine the mayonnaise dressing, red onion, lime juice, ginger, and garlic. Cover and blend until onion is finely chopped and mixture is combined.

2 Place chicken in a medium bowl. Pour the dressing over chicken; toss to coat. If desired, cover and refrigerate up to 1 hour to blend flavors.

3 Divide the celery between two dinner plates. Top with the chicken mixture and sprinkle with pumpkin seeds. If desired, serve with lime wedges

Nutrition Facts per serving: 306 cal., 16 g total fat (3 g sat. fat), 99 mg chol., 276 mg sodium, 7 g carbo., 34 g pro.

crunchy chicken AND FRUIT SALAD

Start to Finish: 20 minutes
Makes: 4 servings

1   2½-pound deli-roasted whole chicken

3   oranges

⅓   cup light mayonnaise

1   5-ounce bag sweet baby lettuces

2   small red and/or green apples, cored and coarsely chopped

¼   cup pecan halves

1 Remove chicken from bones. Tear chicken in bite-size chunks. Set aside.

2 Squeeze juice from 1 orange. Stir enough juice into the mayonnaise to make dressing consistency. Season with black pepper. Peel and section remaining oranges.

3 On salad plates arrange greens, chicken, apples, and oranges. Sprinkle pecan halves. Pass dressing.

Nutrition Facts per serving: 455 cal., 30 g total fat (7 g sat. fat), 132 mg chol., 956 mg sodium, 23 g carbo., 29 g pro.

rotisserie chicken GREEK SALAD

This quick-to-fix salad uses deli-roasted chicken, bottled Greek dressing, packaged greens, and crumbled feta cheese that can be prepared in less than 20 minutes.

Start to Finish: 20 minutes
Makes: 6 main-dish servings

1   **2 to 2½ pounds rotisserie chicken from the deli, whole or cut up**

2   **tablespoons plus ⅓ cup bottled Greek vinaigrette salad dressing**

1   **10-ounce pkg. romaine lettuce salad or 8 cups torn romaine lettuce**

½   **cup small fresh mint leaves, lightly packed**

½   **cup lightly packed small fresh oregano leaves**

   Feta cheese

⅓   **cup kalamata olives, pitted and halved**

   Fresh mint sprigs

   Fresh oregano sprigs

   Lemon wedges

1 Use two forks to pull meat off the bones and shred in large pieces. Discard bones and skin, if desired. Place chicken pieces in a medium bowl. Drizzle with 2 tablespoons of the vinaigrette. Toss well to combine. Let stand 10 minutes.

2 Meanwhile, toss lettuce, mint, and oregano with remaining ⅓ cup Greek vinaigrette. Arrange lettuce on a large serving platter.

3 Arrange chicken in center of greens. Sprinkle with feta cheese and olives. Garnish chicken with mint and oregano sprigs. Serve with lemon wedges.

Nutrition Facts per serving: 297 cal., 21 g total fat (5 g sat. fat), 74 mg chol., 442 mg sodium, 4 g carbo., 23 g pro.

roasted chicken SALAD TOSTADAS

If you want to serve as a tossed salad, combine ingredients in a bowl and crumble the crisp tortilla over the top.

Prep: 35 minutes
Start to Finish: 35 minutes
Makes: 4 servings

1½ **tablespoons olive oil**

2 **teaspoons ground cumin**

8 **(5.5-inch) corn tortillas**

2 **cups shredded purchased roasted chicken**

4 **tablespoons fresh lime juice, plus wedges for garnish**

   Salt and ground black pepper

1 **can (15.5 ounce) black beans, rinsed and drained well**

1 **cup grape tomatoes, quartered**

1 **avocado**

4 **cups thinly sliced romaine lettuce**

1 **cup purchased salsa**

½ **cup low-fat sour cream**

1 Preheat broiler. Whisk together oil and 1½ teaspoons cumin in a small bowl; salt to taste. Lightly brush both sides of each tortilla with cumin oil and arrange in a single layer on a cookie sheet. Broil 4 inches from heat, turning once, until golden brown and crisp, about 2 minutes. Transfer to rack to cool.

2 Meanwhile, toss chicken with 2 tablespoons lime juice in a serving bowl; salt and pepper to taste.

3 Toss together beans, tomatoes, 1 tablespoon lime juice, and remaining ½ teaspoon cumin in another serving bowl; salt and pepper to taste.

4 Halve, pit, peel, and slice avocado. Transfer to a shallow bowl and drizzle with remaining 1 tablespoon lime juice; salt to taste.

5 Arrange bowls of chicken, beans, avocado slices, and stack of tortillas on the table. Place lettuce, salsa, and sour cream in separate bowls; serve on the side with lime wedges. Top each tortilla with desired toppings to create individual salad tostadas.

Nutrition Facts per serving: 475 cal., 22 g total fat (5 g sat. fat), 73 mg chol., 1,114 mg sodium, 51 g carbo., 26 g pro.

sandwiches
AND WRAPS

Cobb Salad Hoagies, *recipe page 76*

sloppy CHICKEN PIZZA JOES

Everyone will love this vegetable-studded chicken take off on the ground beef sloppy sandwiches.

Prep: 15 minutes
Cook: 6 to 8 hours (low) or
      3 to 4 hours (high)
Broil: 1 minute
Makes: 8 sandwiches

Nonstick cooking spray

3 **pounds uncooked ground
   chicken or uncooked ground
   turkey**

2 **14-ounce jars pizza sauce**

2 **cups frozen (yellow, green,
   and red) peppers and onion
   stir-fry vegetables, thawed
   and chopped**

1 **14.5-ounce can diced
   tomatoes**

8 **hoagie rolls, split**

8 **slices mozzarella or
   provolone cheese (8 ounces)**

1 Coat a large skillet with cooking spray. Heat skillet over medium-high heat. Add chicken to hot skillet; cook until chicken is no longer pink, stirring to break apart. In a 3½- or 4-quart slow cooker, combine chicken, pizza sauce, vegetables, and undrained tomatoes.

2 Cover and cook on low-heat setting for 6 to 8 hours or on high-heat setting for 3 to 4 hours.

3 Arrange split rolls, cut sides up, on an unheated broiler pan. Broil 3 to 4 inches from the heat for 1 to 2 minutes or until toasted. Spoon chicken mixture onto bottoms of toasted rolls. Top with cheese and roll tops.

Nutrition Facts per sandwich: 661 cal., 26 g total fat (4 g sat. fat), 135 mg chol., 1,296 mg sodium, 60 g carbo., 47 g pro.

chicken patties ON CROISSANTS

These oval burgers with a tarragon-mayonnaise topping are also great in the round served on hamburger buns.

Prep: 25 minutes
Cook: 10 minutes
Makes: 4 sandwiches

½ **cup mayonnaise or salad dressing**

1 **tablespoon finely chopped green onion**

1 **teaspoon snipped parsley**

⅛ **teaspoon dried tarragon, crushed**

   Dash ground black pepper

1 **beaten egg**

½ **cup finely chopped celery**

½ **cup finely chopped green sweet pepper**

⅓ **cup fine dry seasoned bread crumbs**

2 **tablespoons finely chopped onion**

1 **tablespoon snipped parsley**

1 **teaspoon Worcestershire sauce**

¼ **teaspoon salt**

1 **pound ground raw chicken**

2 **tablespoons cooking oil**

4 **croissants, split lengthwise**

4 **lettuce leaves**

1 **large tomato, sliced**

1 For tarragon sauce, in a small bowl combine mayonnaise, green onion, the 1 teaspoon snipped parsley, tarragon, and pepper. Stir to mix. Cover and chill until serving time.

2 In medium mixing bowl combine egg, celery, green sweet pepper, bread crumbs, onion, the 1 tablespoon snipped parsley, Worcestershire sauce, and salt. Add chicken; mix lightly but well. Shape into four 4-inch oval patties.

3 In large skillet cook chicken patties in hot oil over medium heat for 10 to 12 minutes or until an instant-read thermometer inserted in side of patty registers 165°F, turning once. Spread each cut side of croissants with some of the tarragon sauce. Arrange a lettuce leaf and a chicken patty on bottom half of each croissant. Top each with additional tarragon sauce and croissant top. Serve with tomato slices.

Nutrition Facts per serving: 560 cal., 43 g total fat (10 g sat. fat), 153 mg chol., 610 mg sodium, 23 g carbo., 22 g pro.

Make Ahead: Prepare tarragon sauce up to 24 hours ahead; cover and chill.

plum chicken IN TORTILLAS

Hoisin sauce is a Chinese condiment that can be found in the Asian section of the supermarket. The reddish brown sauce adds a sweet-and-spicy flavor to the chicken.

Prep: 20 minutes
Cook: 4 hours (low) or
       2 hours (high)
Makes: 6 servings

1 **16-ounce can whole, unpitted purple plums, drained**

1 **cup hot-style vegetable juice**

¼ **cup hoisin sauce**

4½ **teaspoons quick-cooking tapioca**

2 **teaspoons grated gingerroot**

½ **teaspoon five-spice powder**

1 **pound skinless, boneless chicken thighs**

6 **7- to 8-inch flour tortillas, warmed**

2 **cups packaged shredded broccoli (broccoli slaw mix) or packaged shredded cabbage with carrot (coleslaw mix)**

1 Remove pits from plums. Place plums in a blender container or food processor bowl. Cover and blend or process until smooth. Transfer plum puree to a 3½- or 4-quart slow cooker. Stir in vegetable juice, hoisin sauce, tapioca, gingerroot, and five-spice powder. Rinse chicken; cut into strips. Stir chicken into slow cooker.

2 Cover; cook on low-heat setting for 4 to 5 hours or on high-heat setting for 2 to 2½ hours. Remove chicken from cooker, reserving juices.

3 Spoon about ⅓ cup chicken mixture onto each warm tortilla just below the center. Drizzle with the reserved juices. Top each with ⅓ cup shredded slaw mix. Roll up tortilla.

Nutrition Facts per serving: 276 cal., 4 g total fat (1 g sat. fat), 44 mg chol., 510 mg sodium, 38 g carbo., 21 g pro.

skillet chicken SALAD PITAS

Prep: 30 minutes
Marinate: 1 hour
Chill: 1 hour
Cook: 8 minutes
Makes: 8 sandwiches

⅓ **cup snipped fresh cilantro**

¼ **cup Asian sweet chili sauce**

4 **tablespoons lime juice**

1 **tablespoon minced garlic**

1 **teaspoon olive oil**

⅛ **teaspoon kosher salt or salt**

2 **pounds skinless, boneless chicken breast halves, cut in 1-inch pieces**

1 **large red sweet pepper, cut into bite-size strips**

⅔ **cup mayonnaise**

½ **cup snipped fresh cilantro**

8 **pita bread rounds**

8 **leaves red or green leaf lettuce**

① In resealable plastic bag set in a shallow dish, combine ⅓ cup cilantro, chili sauce, 2 tablespoons lime juice, garlic, olive oil, and salt. Add chicken. Seal bag and turn to coat. Marinate in the refrigerator for 1 hour.

② Heat a 12-inch skillet over medium-high heat. Add chicken mixture, half at a time, and cook 3 minutes per batch, stirring occasionally. Return all the chicken to the skillet. Add sweet pepper; continue cooking 5 minutes more or until chicken is no longer pink, stirring occasionally. Using a slotted spoon transfer chicken mixture to a large bowl. Cover; refrigerate 1 to 8 hours.

③ For dressing, in a small bowl combine mayonnaise, ½ cup cilantro, and 2 tablespoons lime juice. To serve, top each pita with a lettuce leaf. If necessary, drain excess liquid from the chicken mixture. Spoon chicken mixture on half of each pita. Spoon mayonnaise mixture over chicken. Fold pita in half.

Nutrition Facts per sandwich: 456 cal., 18 g total fat (3 g sat. fat), 73 mg chol., 644 mg sodium, 38 g carbo., 33 g pro.

bbq CHICKEN SANDWICHES

Next time you fix chicken breast halves, cook a couple extra ones and freeze them to have on hand for these delicious supper sandwiches.

Start to Finish: 15 minutes
Makes: 4 servings

2 **cups cooked chicken or turkey breast cut into strips**

½ **cup shredded carrot (1 medium)**

½ **cup bottled barbecue sauce**

1 **16-ounce loaf French bread, split and toasted, or 4 hamburger buns, split and toasted**

½ **cup shredded Monterey Jack cheese (2 ounces) (optional)**

Pickle slices (optional)

1 In a medium saucepan heat the chicken, carrot, and barbecue sauce over medium heat until bubbly.

2 Spoon chicken mixture onto bottom half of bread loaf. If desired, top chicken mixture with cheese. Place on a baking sheet. Broil 3 to 4 inches from heat for 1 to 2 minutes or until cheese melts. If desired, top with pickle slices. Cover with bread top. If using bread, cut into serving-size pieces.

Nutrition Facts per servings: 269 cal., 6 g total fat (2 g sat. fat), 53 mg chol., 520 mg sodium, 27 g carbo., 25 g pro.

pear-chicken MONTE CRISTO SANDWICHES

These golden sandwiches are dipped like French toast and then baked.

Prep: 20 minutes
Bake: 25 minutes
Oven: 350°F
Makes: 4 servings

- 2 to 3 tablespoons prepared horseradish
- 4 thick slices firm-texture white bread
- 4 thin slices mozzarella cheese
- 6 ounces cooked chicken or turkey breast, cut into thin slices
- 1 medium pear, cored, peeled, and thinly sliced
- 1 egg, beaten
- ⅓ cup half-and-half or light cream

1 Spread 1 to 1½ teaspoons horseradish on one side of half the bread slices. Top each with a slice of cheese, a slice of chicken, and several pear slices. Add another slice of cheese and a slice of chicken. Top with a slice of bread.

2 Combine eggs and half-and-half in a shallow dish. Dip both sides of each sandwich in egg mixture; allow each side to stand about 10 seconds until egg mixture is absorbed. Place sandwiches in a greased 15x10x1-inch baking pan.

3 Bake in 350°F oven for 15 minutes. Carefully turn the sandwiches over and bake about 10 minutes more or until bread is golden and cheese is just melted. To serve, slice each sandwich into four triangles.

Nutrition Facts per serving: 271 cal., 11 g total fat (5 g sat. fat), 113 mg chol., 328 mg sodium, 19 g carbo., 24 g pro.

Make Ahead: Assemble the sandwiches and place in baking pan. Cover and refrigerate overnight.

cucumber-chicken PITA SANDWICHES

When it's too hot to cook, try this refreshing sandwich.

Start to Finish: 15 minutes
Makes: 4 servings

½ **cup plain yogurt**

¼ **cup finely chopped cucumber**

½ **teaspoon dried dill**

¼ **teaspoon dried mint, crushed**

4 **large pita bread rounds**

4 **lettuce leaves**

6 **ounces thinly sliced cooked chicken breast**

1 **small tomato, thinly sliced**

⅓ **cup crumbled feta cheese**

1 For dressing, in a small bowl stir together yogurt, cucumber, dill, and mint. Set aside.

2 For each sandwich, place a pita bread round on a plate. Top with lettuce, chicken, tomato, and feta cheese. Spoon dressing on top. Roll up pita bread; secure with wooden toothpicks. Serve immediately.

Nutrition Facts per serving: 377 cal., 14 g total fat (5 g sat. fat), 55 mg chol., 793 mg sodium, 43 g carbo., 18 g pro.

parmesan chicken SALAD SANDWICHES

Start to Finish: 10 minutes
Makes: 6 main-dish servings

½ cup low-fat mayonnaise

1 tablespoon lemon juice

2 teaspoons snipped fresh basil

2½ cups chopped cooked chicken
    or turkey

¼ cup grated Parmesan cheese

¼ cup thinly sliced green onions

3 tablespoons finely chopped
    celery

Salt and ground black pepper

1 For dressing, in a small bowl stir together mayonnaise, lemon juice and basil. Set aside.

2 For salad, in a medium bowl combine chicken, Parmesan cheese, green onions, and celery. Pour dressing over chicken mixture; toss to coat. Season to taste with salt and ground black pepper. Serve immediately or cover and chill in the refrigerator for 1 to 4 hours. Serve on toasted wheat bread.

Nutrition Facts per serving: 194 cal., 12 g total fat (3 g sat. fat), 61 mg chol., 366 mg sodium, 2 g carbo., 18 g pro.

cobb salad HOAGIES

Start to Finish: 35 minutes
Makes: 4 sandwiches

3 tablespoons olive oil

1 tablespoon white wine
   vinegar

1 teaspoon Dijon-style mustard

½ teaspoon salt

½ teaspoon ground black
   pepper

1 medium avocado, seeded,
   peeled, and finely chopped

1⅓ cups cubed cooked chicken
   (about 7 ounces)

2 roma tomatoes, chopped

½ cup crumbled blue cheese
   (2 ounces)

4 slices bacon, crisp-cooked,
   drained, and crumbled

4 hoagie buns, split, hollowed
   out, and toasted

4 Boston or Bibb lettuce leaves

2 hard-cooked eggs, chopped

1 For dressing, in small bowl whisk together oil, vinegar, mustard, salt, and pepper. Stir in avocado. Set aside.

2 In medium bowl combine chicken, tomatoes, blue cheese, and bacon. Pour dressing over chicken mixture; toss gently to coat.

3 Line bottom halves of buns with lettuce. Fill with chicken mixture and hard-cooked egg. Replace top halves of buns.

Nutrition Facts per sandwich: 659 cal., 35 g total fat (9 g sat. fat), 165 mg chol., 1,214 mg sodium, 55 g carbo., 32 g pro.

fruity chicken salad
SANDWICHES

Makes: 4 servings

- **2 cups chopped cooked chicken breast (10 ounces)**
- **1 small Red Delicious or Granny Smith apple, cored and chopped**
- **⅓ cup sliced celery**
- **¼ cup raisins**
- **1 green onion, thinly sliced**
- **¼ cup plain fat-free yogurt**
- **¼ cup bottled reduced-calorie ranch salad dressing**
- **Red-tipped leaf lettuce**
- **8 slices whole wheat or other bread**

1 In a large bowl stir together the chicken, apple, celery, raisins, and green onion. In a small bowl combine yogurt and ranch salad dressing. Pour over chicken mixture; toss gently to coat.

2 Arrange lettuce leaves on half of the bread slices. Spread chicken mixture on lettuce. Top with the remaining bread.

Nutrition Facts per serving: 332 cal., 8 g total fat (1 g sat. fat), 65 mg chol., 590 mg sodium, 38 g carbo., 29 g pro.

honey-chicken SANDWICHES

Buttery, flaky biscuits hold the moist, warm honey-and-chicken filling making a wonderful main dish for a special luncheon or for a special family treat.

Start to Finish: 20 minutes
Makes: 4 servings

- 3 **tablespoons honey**
- 2 **teaspoons snipped fresh thyme or ½ teaspoon dried thyme, crushed**
- 1 **small red onion, halved and thinly sliced**
- 12 **ounces cut-up cooked chicken**
- 4 **baked biscuits, split**

1 In a medium skillet combine honey and thyme; stir in red onion. Cook and stir over medium-low heat just until hot (do not boil). Stir in chicken; heat through. Arrange chicken mixture on biscuit bottoms. Add tops.

Nutrition Facts per serving: 342 cal., 12 g total fat (3 g sat. fat), 76 mg chol., 443 mg sodium, 31 g carbo., 27 g pro.

chicken olive CALZONES

Whether served warm with spaghetti sauce or at room temperature from a lunch bag, these pizza-flavor sandwiches will be a family favorite.

Prep: 25 minutes
Bake: 10 minutes
Oven: 425°F
Stand: 5 minutes
Makes: 6 calzones

- 1½ **cups chopped cooked chicken (8 ounces)**
- ½ **cup shredded Monterey Jack cheese (2 ounces)**
- ¼ **cup chopped celery**
- ¼ **cup chopped pitted ripe olives**
- ½ **teaspoon dried basil, crushed**
- ¼ **teaspoon dried oregano, crushed**
- ⅛ **teaspoon garlic powder**
- ⅛ **teaspoon ground black pepper**
- ⅓ **cup tub-style cream cheese with chives and onion**
- 1 **13.8-ounce package refrigerated pizza dough**
- 1 **egg, lightly beaten**
- 1 **tablespoon water**
- **Grated Parmesan cheese (optional)**
- **Spaghetti sauce, warmed (optional)**

1 Preheat oven to 425°F. For filling, in a medium bowl combine chicken, Monterey Jack cheese, celery, olives, basil, oregano, garlic powder, and pepper. Stir in cream cheese. Set aside.

2 For calzones, unroll pizza dough. On lightly floured surface, roll dough into a 15x10-inch rectangle. Cut into six 5-inch squares. Divide chicken-olive filling among the squares. Brush edges with water. Lift one corner and stretch dough over to the opposite corner. Seal edges of dough well with tines of a fork. Arrange calzones on a greased baking sheet. Prick tops with a fork. In a small bowl combine egg and 1 tablespoon water; brush over the calzones. If desired, sprinkle with Parmesan cheese.

3 Bake for 10 to 12 minutes or until golden. Let stand for 5 minutes before serving. If desired, serve with warm spaghetti sauce.

Nutrition Facts per calzone: 268 cal., 13 g total fat (5 g sat. fat), 90 mg chol., 320 mg sodium, 19 g carbo., 18 g pro.

chutney-chicken SALAD SANDWICHES

Start to Finish: 20 minutes
Makes: 4 servings

¼ **cup mango chutney**

2 **tablespoons mayonnaise or salad dressing, or plain low-fat yogurt**

1 **teaspoon curry powder**

2 **cups cubed, cooked chicken or turkey**

1 **cup seedless red grapes, halved**

¼ **cup sliced or slivered almonds, toasted**

4 **croissants, split, or 6-inch pita bread rounds, halved crosswise**

Lettuce leaves

① Cut up any large pieces of chutney. Combine chutney, mayonnaise, and curry powder. Stir in chicken, grapes, and almonds.

② Line croissants with lettuce; top with chicken mixture.

Nutrition Facts per serving: 547 cal., 27 g total fat (9 g sat. fat), 103 mg chol., 541 mg sodium, 49 g carbo., 27 g pro.

smoked CHICKEN AND PROSCIUTTO PANINI

Prep: 25 minutes
Grill: 6 minutes per batch
Makes: 4 sandwiches

½ **cup mayonnaise or salad dressing**

¼ **cup bottled roasted red sweet pepper, drained and patted dry with paper towels**

1 **clove garlic, quartered**

4 **soft French or sourdough rolls (about 7x3 inches)**

8 **ounces thinly sliced smoked chicken or smoked turkey**

2 **ounces thinly sliced prosciutto**

8 **ounces sliced provolone or mozzarella cheese**

1 **cup mesclun or baby lettuce**

1 In a food processor or blender combine mayonnaise, red pepper, and garlic. Blend or process until mixture is almost smooth.

2 Preheat an electric sandwich press, a covered indoor grill, a grill pan, or a skillet. To assemble sandwiches, split each roll in half horizontally; spread cut sides of rolls with the mayonnaise mixture. Layer chicken, prosciutto, cheese, and mesclun on bottom halves of rolls. Replace top halves of rolls.

3 Place sandwiches (half at a time, if necessary) in the sandwich press or indoor grill; cover and cook about 6 minutes or until cheese melts and rolls are toasted. (If using a grill pan or skillet, place sandwiches on grill pan. Weight sandwiches down and grill about 2 minutes or until rolls are lightly toasted. Turn sandwiches over, weight down, and grill until remaining side is lightly toasted.)

Nutrition Facts per sandwich: 842 cal., 49 g total fat (17 g sat. fat), 111 mg chol., 2,465 mg sodium, 59 g carbo., 38 g pro.

chicken focaccia SANDWICHES

On the next sunny day, fill your cooler with these hearty sandwiches, a few pieces of fresh fruit, and a beverage to take on a picnic to the park.

Start to Finish: 15 minutes
Makes: 6 sandwich wedges

1　**8-inch tomato or onion Italian flatbread (focaccia) or 1 loaf sourdough bread**

⅓　**cup light mayonnaise dressing or salad dressing**

1　**cup lightly packed fresh basil leaves**

2　**cups sliced or shredded deli-roasted chicken**

½　**of a 7-ounce jar roasted red sweet peppers, drained and cut into strips (about ½ cup)**

1 Using a long serrated knife, cut bread in half horizontally. Spread cut sides of bread halves with mayonnaise dressing.

2 Layer basil leaves, chicken, and roasted sweet peppers between bread halves. Cut into wedges.

Nutrition Facts per serving: 263 cal., 10 g total fat (2 g sat. fat), 51 mg chol., 341 mg sodium, 27 g carbo., 19 g pro.

pulled CHICKEN SANDWICHES

Prep: 25 minutes
Cook: 7 minutes
Makes: 6 sandwiches

1 2- to 2¼-pound deli-roasted chicken

1 tablespoon olive oil

1 medium onion, cut into ¼-inch-thick slices

⅓ cup cider vinegar or white wine vinegar

½ cup tomato sauce

3 to 4 tablespoons seeded and finely chopped fresh red and/or green hot chile peppers*

2 tablespoons snipped fresh thyme

2 tablespoons molasses

2 tablespoons water

½ teaspoon salt

4 sandwich buns, split

Bread-and-butter pickle slices

1 Remove meat from chicken (discard skin and bones). Use two forks or your fingers to pull meat into shreds.

2 In a large skillet heat the olive oil over medium heat. Add onion; cook about 5 minutes or until tender, stirring occasionally to separate into rings. Add vinegar; cook and stir 1 minute more.

3 Stir in tomato sauce, chile peppers, thyme, molasses, water, and salt. Bring to boiling. Add the chicken; tossing gently to coat. Heat through. Serve on rolls with pickle slices.

Nutrition Facts per serving: 445 cal., 12 g total fat (3 g sat. fat), 84 mg chol., 990 mg sodium, 51 g carbo., 33 g pro.

***Note:** Because chile peppers contain volatile oils that can burn your skin and eyes, avoid direct contact with them as much as possible. When working with chile peppers, wear plastic or rubber gloves. If your bare hands do touch the peppers, wash your hands and nails well with soap and warm water.

thai CHICKEN-BROCCOLI WRAPS

Another time, make the peanut sauce to serve as a dipping sauce with take-out fried chicken strips.

Start to Finish: 20 minutes
Makes: 6 servings

6   8- to 10-inch plain, red, and/or green flour tortillas
½   teaspoon garlic salt
¼   to ½ teaspoon pepper
¾   pound skinless, boneless chicken breast strips for stir-frying
1   tablespoon cooking oil
4   cups packaged shredded broccoli (broccoli slaw mix)
1   medium red onion, cut into thin wedges
1   teaspoon grated fresh ginger
    Peanut Sauce*

1 Wrap tortillas in paper towels. Microwave on high power for 30 seconds to soften. (Or wrap tortillas in foil. Heat in a 350°F oven for 10 minutes.)

2 In a small bowl combine garlic salt and pepper. Add chicken; toss to coat evenly. In a large skillet cook and stir seasoned chicken in hot oil over medium-high heat for 2 to 3 minutes or until cooked through. Remove from skillet; keep warm. Add broccoli, onion, and ginger to skillet. Cook and stir for 2 to 3 minutes or until vegetables are crisp-tender.

3 To assemble, spread each tortilla with about 1 tablespoon Peanut Sauce. Top with chicken strips and vegetable mixture. Roll up each tortilla, securing with a toothpick. Serve immediately with remaining sauce.

*Peanut Sauce: In a small saucepan combine ¼ cup sugar, ¼ cup creamy peanut butter, 3 tablespoons soy sauce, 3 tablespoons water, 2 tablespoons cooking oil, and 1 teaspoon bottled minced garlic. Heat until sugar is dissolved, stirring frequently. Makes about ⅔ cup.

Nutrition Facts per serving: 330 cal., 16 g total fat (3 g sat. fat), 30 mg chol., 911 mg sodium, 30 g carbo., 17 g pro.

fajita-ranch CHICKEN WRAPS

Start to Finish: 20 minutes
Makes: 4 servings

12 ounces skinless, boneless chicken breast strips for stir-frying

½ teaspoon chili powder

¼ teaspoon garlic powder

  Nonstick cooking spray

1 small red, yellow, or green sweet pepper, seeded and cut into thin strips

2 tablespoons bottled reduced-calorie ranch salad dressing

2 10-inch whole wheat, tomato, jalapeño, or plain flour tortillas, warmed*

½ cup Easy Fresh Salsa**

⅓ cup reduced-fat shredded cheddar cheese

① Sprinkle chicken strips with chili powder and garlic powder. Coat a medium nonstick skillet with nonstick spray; heat over medium-high heat. Cook chicken and sweet pepper strips in hot skillet over medium heat for 4 to 6 minutes or until chicken is no longer pink and pepper strips are tender. Drain if necessary. Toss with salad dressing.

② Divide chicken and pepper mixture between warmed tortillas. Top with Easy Fresh Salsa and cheese. Roll up; cut in half.

*To warm tortillas: Wrap tortillas tightly in foil. Heat in a 350°F oven about 10 minutes or until heated through.

**Easy Fresh Salsa: In a medium bowl combine 2 seeded and chopped tomatoes, ¼ cup finely chopped red onion, ¼ cup chopped yellow or green sweet pepper, 2 to 3 teaspoons snipped fresh cilantro, ½ teaspoon minced garlic, ⅛ teaspoon salt, a dash of black pepper, and, if desired, a few drops bottled hot pepper sauce. Serve immediately or cover and chill for up to 3 days. Stir before serving. Makes: 1⅔ cups.

Nutrition Facts per serving: 224 cal., 7 g total fat (2 g sat. fat), 59 mg chol., 316 mg sodium, 15 g carbo., 25 g pro.

chicken AND BLACK BEAN WRAP

Start to Finish: 10 minutes
Makes: 4 servings

½ **cup Black Bean-Smoked Chile Dip***

4 **7- or 8-inch whole wheat flour tortillas**

12 **ounces cooked skinless chicken or turkey breast, chopped (about 2⅓ cups)**

4 **cups shredded or torn romaine or whole fresh baby spinach leaves**

1 **cup coarsely snipped fresh cilantro**

¼ **cup purchased salsa**

1 Spread Black Bean-Smoked Chile Dip on one side of each tortilla. Top with chicken, romaine, cilantro, and salsa. Roll up tortillas. If desired, secure with toothpicks.

*Black Bean-Smoked Chile Dip: In a small saucepan heat 1 tablespoon canola oil over medium heat. Add ¾ cup finely chopped onion, 1 teaspoon ground coriander, and 1 teaspoon ground cumin; cover and cook about 10 minutes or until very tender, stirring occasionally. Remove from heat; stir in ¼ cup snipped fresh cilantro. Transfer onion mixture to a blender or food processor. Add one 15-ounce can black beans, rinsed and drained; ½ cup water; 1 tablespoon lime juice; 1 teaspoon finely chopped chipotle chile pepper in adobo sauce;** and ⅛ teaspoon salt. Cover and blend or process until nearly smooth. Serve immediately or cover and chill for up to 3 days before serving. Makes: 1⅔ cups.

Nutrition Facts per serving: 324 cal., 8 g total fat (2 g sat. fat), 72 mg chol., 600 mg sodium, 24 g carbo., 38 g pro.

**Note: Because chile peppers contain volatile oils that can burn your skin and eyes, avoid direct contact with them as much as possible. When working with chile peppers, wear plastic or rubber gloves. If your bare hands do touch the peppers, wash your hands and nails well with soap and warm water.

southwest CHICKEN WRAPS

This is a fun way to serve chicken strips and can easily be made into a meal-to-go if you omit the salsa.

Makes: 6 servings

½ **of a 28-ounce package frozen cooked, breaded chicken strips (about 24 strips)**

½ **of an 8-ounce tub light cream cheese**

1 **green onion, thinly sliced**

1 **tablespoon snipped fresh cilantro**

6 **7- to 8-inch flour tortillas**

1 **red sweet pepper, seeded and cut into bite-size strips**

½ **cup shredded reduced-fat or regular Monterey Jack cheese (2 ounces)**

Bottled salsa (optional)

1 Bake chicken strips according to package directions.

2 Meanwhile, in a small bowl stir together cream cheese, green onion, and cilantro. Spread over tortillas. Top with pepper strips and cheese. Top with hot chicken strips. Roll up tortillas around filling. Cut in half to serve. Secure tortillas shut with toothpicks. Serve with salsa, if desired.

Nutrition Facts per serving: 356 cal., 20 g total fat (6 g sat. fat), 54 mg chol., 610 mg sodium, 27 g carbo., 18 g pro.

cilantro-lime CHICKEN WRAPS

Start to Finish: 25 minutes
Oven: 350°F
Makes: 6 servings

6   10-inch whole grain flour
    tortillas

1   15.25-ounce can whole kernel
    corn, drained

1   15-ounce can black beans,
    rinsed and drained

2   6-ounce packages
    refrigerated chopped cooked
    chicken breast

1   cup purchased lime and garlic
    salsa

1   teaspoon dried cilantro,
    crushed

4   cups packaged mixed salad
    greens with carrots, red
    cabbage, radishes, and snow
    peas or other mixed greens

    Purchased lime and garlic
    salsa (optional)

1 Preheat oven to 350°F. Stack tortillas and wrap tightly in foil. Heat in oven for 10 minutes to soften.

2 Meanwhile, in a medium saucepan combine corn, black beans, chicken, the 1 cup salsa, and the cilantro. Cook over medium heat about 5 minutes or until heated through.

3 Divide salad greens among tortillas. Top with corn mixture. Roll up tortillas. If desired, serve with additional salsa.

Nutrition Facts per serving: 326 cal., 4 g total fat (1 g sat. fat), 40 mg chol., 1,606 mg sodium, 53 g carbo., 22 g pro.

curried chicken SALAD WRAPS

Prep: 20 minutes
Chill: 2 to 24 hours
Makes: 4 servings

½ **cup fat-free or low-fat mayonnaise or salad dressing**

½ **teaspoon curry powder**

⅛ **teaspoon ground black pepper**

2 **cups chopped cooked chicken breast (about 10 ounces)**

¼ **cup sliced green onions**

4 **romaine leaves or 8 fresh spinach leaves**

4 **7-inch whole wheat flour tortillas**

1 **medium tomato, chopped**

1 In a medium bowl combine mayonnaise dressing, curry powder, and pepper. Stir in chicken and green onions. Cover and chill for 2 to 24 hours.

2 To assemble, place 1 romaine leaf or 2 spinach leaves on each tortilla. Top with chicken mixture and tomatoes. Roll up; cut in half to serve.

Nutrition Facts per serving: 246 cal., 5 g total fat (1 g sat. fat), 60 mg chol., 537 mg sodium, 18 g carbo., 28 g pro.

baked
AND ROASTED

Chicken with Basil Cream Sauce, *recipe page 99*

baked PARMESAN CHICKEN

Crushed cereal and cheese enrobe boneless chicken breasts for a short prep main dish that is long on flavor.

Prep: 10 minutes
Bake: 30 minutes
Oven: 375°F
Makes: 4 servings

3 tablespoons butter or margarine, melted

½ cup crushed cornflakes

2 tablespoons grated Parmesan cheese

¼ teaspoon dried Italian seasoning, crushed

4 skinless, boneless chicken breast halves (about 1¼ pounds total)

1 Preheat oven to 375°F. Pour melted butter into a shallow dish. In another shallow dish combine cornflakes, cheese, and Italian seasoning. Dip chicken into melted butter, then into cornflake mixture, turning to coat.

2 Place chicken on a roasting rack in a shallow baking pan. Bake, uncovered, about 30 minutes or until chicken is no longer pink (170°F).

Nutrition Facts per serving: 287 cal., 12 g total fat (7 g sat. fat), 109 mg chol., 318 mg sodium, 9 g carbo., 35 g pro.

chicken WITH BASIL CREAM SAUCE

Use fresh basil for this recipe if you have it. It will give the sauce a brighter, more intense flavor than dried basil.

Start to Finish: 30 minutes
Oven: 400°F
Makes: 4 servings

¼ **cup fine dry bread crumbs**

1 **tablespoon snipped fresh basil or ¾ teaspoon dried basil, crushed**

⅛ **teaspoon ground black pepper**

⅛ **teaspoon paprika**

1 **tablespoon butter, melted**

4 **skinless, boneless chicken breast halves (about 1¼ pounds total)**

⅔ **cup milk**

2 **teaspoons all-purpose flour**

¾ **teaspoon instant chicken bouillon granules**

1 Preheat oven to 400°F. In a small bowl stir together bread crumbs, 2 teaspoons of the fresh basil (or ½ teaspoon of the dried basil) the pepper, and paprika. Add melted butter; toss to coat.

2 Arrange chicken in a 2-quart rectangular baking dish. Sprinkle chicken with the crumb mixture, pressing onto the chicken to coat. Bake for 20 to 25 minutes or until chicken is no longer pink (170°F).

3 Meanwhile, in a small saucepan stir together milk, flour, bouillon granules, and remaining ¼ teaspoon dried basil (if using) until combined. Cook and stir until thickened and bubbly. Cook and stir for 1 minute more. Stir in remaining 1 teaspoon fresh basil (if using). Serve over chicken.

Nutrition Facts per serving: 238 cal., 6 g total fat (3 g sat. fat), 93 mg chol., 460 mg sodium, 8 g carbo., 35 g pro.

chicken STUFFED WITH SMOKED MOZZARELLA

Prep: 40 minutes
Bake: 25 minutes
Oven: 400°F
Makes: 6 servings

6 skinless, boneless chicken breast halves (about 1½ pounds total)

Salt and ground black pepper

¼ cup finely chopped shallots or onions

1 clove garlic, minced

2 teaspoons olive oil

½ of a 10-ounce package frozen chopped spinach, thawed and well drained

3 tablespoons pine nuts or walnuts, toasted

¾ cup shredded smoked mozzarella cheese

¼ cup seasoned fine dry bread crumbs

¼ cup grated Parmesan cheese

1 tablespoon olive oil

1 Place 1 chicken breast half between two pieces of plastic wrap. Pound lightly with the flat side of a meat mallet into a rectangle about ⅛ inch thick. Remove plastic wrap. Season with salt and pepper. Repeat process with all chicken breasts.

2 For filling, in a medium skillet cook shallots and garlic in the 2 teaspoons hot oil until tender. Remove from heat; stir in spinach, nuts, and smoked mozzarella.

3 In a shallow bowl combine bread crumbs and Parmesan cheese.

4 Fill each roll, using 2 to 3 tablespoons of filling.

5 Lightly brush each roll with the 1 tablespoon olive oil; coat with bread crumb mixture. Place rolls, seam sides down, in a shallow baking pan. Bake, uncovered, in a 400°F oven about 25 minutes or until chicken is tender and no longer pink. Remove toothpicks before serving.

Nutrition Facts per serving: 274 cal., 11 g total fat (3 g sat. fat), 77 mg chol., 368 mg sodium, 6 g carbo., 35 g pro.

oven-fried CHICKEN BREASTS

Bake: 20 minutes
Oven: 400°F
Makes: 6 servings

6   skinless, boneless chicken breast halves (about 2 pounds total)
1   cup buttermilk
    Olive oil nonstick cooking spray
1¼ cups crushed cornflakes
1   teaspoon garlic powder or dried minced garlic
1   teaspoon onion powder or dried minced onion
1   teaspoon paprika
½   teaspoon ground black pepper

1 In a large resealable plastic bag combine chicken and buttermilk. Seal bag; turn to coat chicken. Marinate in the refrigerator for 2 to 8 hours, turning occasionally.

2 Preheat oven to 400°F. Line a baking sheet with foil; coat foil with nonstick cooking spray. Drain chicken, discarding excess buttermilk.

3 In another large resealable plastic bag combine crushed cornflakes, garlic, onion, paprika, and pepper; seal bag. Shake well to combine. Add chicken, one piece at a time, and shake the bag to coat the chicken well.

4 Place chicken on the prepared baking sheet. Coat chicken with nonstick cooking spray. Bake, uncovered, for 20 to 25 minutes or until chicken is no longer pink (170°F).

Nutrition Facts per serving: 267 cal., 2 g total fat (1 g sat. fat), 88 mg chol., 336 mg sodium, 23 g carbo., 37 g pro.

blackened chicken WITH
AVOCADO SALSA

Start to Finish: 25 minutes
Oven: 375°F
Makes: 4 servings

4 skinless, boneless chicken
  breast halves (1¼ to
  1½ pounds total)

2 teaspoons blackened steak
  seasoning

1 tablespoon olive oil

2 tablespoons rice vinegar

2 tablespoons olive oil

¼ teaspoon ground cumin

⅛ teaspoon salt

  Dash black pepper

1 avocado, halved, seeded,
  peeled, and chopped

⅔ cup chopped fresh or
  refrigerated papaya

⅓ cup finely chopped red sweet
  pepper

¼ cup chopped fresh cilantro

  Fresh cilantro sprigs
  (optional)

① Preheat oven to 375°F. Lightly sprinkle both sides of chicken breast halves with blackened steak seasoning. In a large ovenproof skillet heat the 1 tablespoon oil on medium heat. Add chicken; cook until browned, turning once. Bake about 15 minutes or until the chicken is no longer pink (170°F).

② Meanwhile, for salsa, in a large bowl whisk together rice vinegar, the 2 tablespoons oil, the cumin, salt, and black pepper. Stir in avocado, papaya, sweet pepper, and chopped cilantro. Serve salsa with chicken. If desired, garnish with cilantro sprigs.

Nutrition Facts per serving: 322 cal., 17 g total fat (3 g sat. fat), 82 mg chol., 513 mg sodium, 7 g carbo., 34 g pro.

chicken PASTA CASSEROLE

Prep: 30 minutes
Bake: 35 minutes
Oven: 350°F
Makes: 5 or 6 servings

8 **ounces dried bow-tie pasta**

2 **tablespoons olive oil**

1 **tablespoon minced garlic (6 cloves)**

1 **pound skinless, boneless chicken breast halves, cut into 1-inch pieces**

1 **teaspoon dried basil, crushed**

½ **teaspoon salt**

¼ **teaspoon ground black pepper**

1 **medium onion, chopped**

1 **small red sweet pepper, chopped**

1 **cup frozen cut asparagus**

1 **8-ounce tub cream cheese spread with chive and onion**

¾ **cup half-and-half, light cream, or milk**

½ **cup panko (Japanese-style bread crumbs)**

¼ **cup sliced almonds**

1 **tablespoon butter, melted**

1 Preheat oven to 350°F. Cook pasta according to package directions; drain. Return pasta to pan.

2 Meanwhile, in a large skillet heat oil; add garlic and cook for 30 seconds. Season chicken with basil, salt, and pepper. Add chicken to the skillet; cook 3 minutes or until no pink remains. Remove from skillet. Add onion and sweet pepper to skillet; cook until tender. Stir in asparagus and cooked chicken. Remove from heat and set aside.

3 Stir cheese into pasta until melted. Stir in chicken mixture and cream. Transfer to a 2-quart rectangular baking dish. In a small bowl combine bread crumbs, almonds, and butter; sprinkle over casserole.

4 Bake, uncovered, for 35 minutes or until heated through.

Nutrition Facts per serving: 615 cal., 31 g total fat (16 g sat. fat), 116 mg chol., 531 mg sodium, 48 g carbo., 33 g pro.

spicy CHICKEN PIZZA

Prep: 25 minutes
Bake: 13 minutes
Oven: 400°F
Makes: 6 servings

12 ounces skinless, boneless chicken breasts, cut into thin strips

2 teaspoons cooking oil

1 medium red sweet pepper, cut into thin strips

½ of a medium red onion, thinly sliced

Nonstick cooking spray

1 10-ounce package refrigerated pizza dough

½ cup bottled mild picante sauce

½ cup shredded sharp cheddar cheese (2 ounces)

1 In a large nonstick skillet cook chicken strips in hot oil over medium-high heat about 5 minutes or until no longer pink. Remove from skillet. Add sweet pepper and onion to skillet; cook about 5 minutes or until tender. Remove from skillet; set aside.

2 Coat a 15x10x1-inch baking pan with nonstick cooking spray. Unroll pizza dough into pan; press with fingers to form a 12x8-inch rectangle. Pinch edges of dough to form crust.

3 Spread crust with picante sauce. Top with chicken and vegetables; sprinkle with cheddar cheese. Bake in a 400°F oven for 13 to 18 minutes or until crust is brown and cheese is melted.

Nutrition Facts per serving: 305 cal., 9 g total fat (3 g sat. fat), 43 mg chol., 527 mg sodium, 34 g carbo., 21 g pro.

chicken-biscuit PIE

Prep: 15 minutes
Bake: 10 minutes
Oven: 450°F
Makes: 4 servings

- **1 10.75-ounce can condensed cream of chicken soup**
- **½ cup milk**
- **¼ cup dairy sour cream**
- **1 cup cubed cooked chicken or turkey (5 ounces)**
- **1½ cups frozen mixed vegetables**
- **½ teaspoon dried basil, crushed**
- **⅛ teaspoon ground black pepper**
- **1 package (5 or 6) refrigerated biscuits, quartered**

1 Preheat oven to 450°F. Lightly grease a 1½-quart casserole; set aside. In a medium saucepan stir together soup, milk, and sour cream. Stir in chicken, mixed vegetables, basil, and pepper. Cook and stir over medium heat until boiling.

2 Spoon chicken mixture into the prepared casserole. Top with quartered biscuits.

3 Bake, uncovered, in the preheated oven for 10 to 12 minutes or until biscuits are light brown.

Nutrition Facts per serving: 335 cal., 14 g total fat (5 g sat. fat), 49 mg chol., 1,049 mg sodium, 33 g carbo., 20 g pro.

nacho CHICKEN CASSEROLE

Prep: 20 minutes
Bake: 38 minutes
Stand: 10 minutes
Oven: 350°F
Makes: 8 servings

1 medium green sweet pepper, chopped

1 medium onion, chopped

2 teaspoons chili powder

½ teaspoon ground cumin

1 tablespoon olive oil

1 10.75-ounce can reduced-fat and reduced-sodium condensed cream of mushroom soup

1 10.75-ounce can reduced-fat and reduced-sodium condensed cream of chicken soup

1 10-ounce can diced tomatoes and green chile peppers, undrained

3 cups coarsely crushed tortilla chips

3 cups cubed cooked chicken

2 cups shredded cheddar cheese (8 ounces)

1 cup whole chips

Assorted toppings (such as thin tomato wedges, sliced pitted ripe olives, and/or sliced green onion) (optional)

Dairy sour cream and/or frozen avocado dip (guacamole), thawed (optional)

1 Preheat oven to 350°F. In a large skillet cook sweet pepper, onion, chili powder, and cumin in hot oil until vegetables are tender. Remove from heat. Stir in cream of mushroom soup, cream of chicken soup, and tomatoes and chile peppers.

2 To assemble, sprinkle 1½ cups of the crushed tortilla chips over bottom of ungreased 2½- to 3-quart oval baking dish. Top with half of the chicken, half of the soup mixture, half of the cheese, and 1 cup of the crushed chips. Top with remaining chicken, remaining soup mixture, and remaining crushed chips.

3 Bake about 35 minutes or until mixture is bubbly around edges and center is heated through. Sprinkle with remaining cheese. Bake for 3 to 4 minutes more or until cheese is melted.

4 Top with whole tortilla chips and, if desired, assorted toppings. Let stand for 10 minutes before serving. If desired, serve with sour cream and/or avocado dip.

Nutrition Facts per serving: 359 cal., 20 g total fat (8 g sat. fat), 81 mg chol., 765 mg sodium, 19 g carbo., 25 g pro.

layered chicken AND CHILE CASSEROLE

Patterned after a popular Texas recipe, this irresistible main dish includes seasoned chicken layered with chile peppers, tortillas, sour cream sauce, and cheese.

Prep: 20 minutes
Bake: 35 minutes
Stand: 10 minutes
Oven: 350°F
Makes: 12 servings

- 2 **tomatillos**
- 1 **cup chopped onion**
- 2 **(about ½ cup) tomatillo, husks**
- 4 **teaspoons chili powder**
- 2 **cloves garlic, minced**
- 2 **tablespoons cooking oil**
- 2 **10¾-ounce cans condensed cream of chicken soup**
- 2 **4-ounce cans diced green chile peppers, drained**
- 2 **4-ounce jars diced pimientos, drained**
- ½ **cup dairy sour cream**
- 12 **6-inch corn tortillas, torn**
- 3 **cups cubed cooked chicken**
- 2 **cups (8 ounces) shredded Monterey Jack cheese**
  Green salsa (optional)

1 Remove and discard the thin, brown, papery husks from the tomatillos. Rinse tomatillos; finely chop (you should have about ½ cup). For sauce, in a medium saucepan cook chopped tomatillos, onion, chili powder, and garlic in hot oil over medium heat until vegetables are tender. Remove from heat; stir in soup, chile peppers, pimientos, and sour cream.

2 Spread ½ cup of the sauce in the bottom of a 3-quart rectangular baking dish. Arrange half of the torn corn tortillas over the sauce. Layer with half of the chicken, half of the remaining sauce, and half of the Monterey Jack cheese. Repeat layers.

3 Bake, covered, in a 350°F oven for 35 to 40 minutes or until heated through. Let stand for 10 minutes before serving. If desired, serve with green salsa.

Nutrition Facts per serving: 297 cal., 16 g total fat (7 g sat. fat), 55 mg chol., 663 mg sodium, 20 g carbo., 19 g pro.

hot and cheesy CHICKEN CASSEROLE

Bake: 35 minutes
Oven: 350°F
Makes: 8 to 10 servings

3   cups chopped cooked chicken

1   14-ounce pkg. frozen broccoli
    florets

2   cups cooked rice*

1½ cups frozen peas

1   10.75-ounce can condensed
    cream of chicken soup

1   10.75-ounce can condensed
    fiesta nacho cheese soup

1   10- to 10.5-ounce can diced
    tomatoes and green chiles

½   cup milk

½   teaspoon crushed red pepper
    (optional)

½   cup shredded cheddar cheese
    (2 ounces)

½   cup shredded mozzarella
    cheese (2 ounces)

1   cup crushed rich round
    crackers

1 Preheat oven to 350°F. Place chicken in bottom of a 13x9x2-inch baking dish or 3-quart rectangular casserole. In large bowl combine broccoli, rice, and peas. Spread mixture over the chicken. In medium bowl combine cream of chicken soup, nacho cheese soup, diced tomatoes and green chiles, milk, and crushed red pepper (if desired). Stir in ¼ cup of the cheddar cheese and ¼ cup of the mozzarella cheese. Pour mixture over broccoli mixture in baking dish. Sprinkle crushed crackers evenly over all. Top with remaining cheddar and mozzarella cheeses.

2 Bake, uncovered, 35 to 40 minutes or until topping is golden.

Nutrition Facts per serving: 354 cal., 15 g total fat (6 g sat. fat), 65 mg chol., 886 mg sodium, 29 g carbo., 26 g pro.

*Note: If you do not have leftover rice, cook ⅔ cup long grain white rice or brown rice in 1⅓ cups boiling water for 15 minutes (40 minutes for brown rice) or until water is absorbed.

swiss CHICKEN BUNDLES

Bake: 30 minutes
Oven: 375°F
Makes: 8 servings

8 dried lasagna noodles

1 beaten egg

2 cups ricotta cheese or
   cream-style cottage cheese,
   drained

1½ cups chopped cooked chicken
   or turkey

1½ teaspoons snipped fresh
   tarragon or basil or
   ¼ teaspoon dried tarragon
   or basil, crushed

2 tablespoons margarine or
   butter

2 tablespoons all-purpose flour

½ teaspoon dry mustard

¼ teaspoon salt

⅛ teaspoon pepper

1½ cups milk

1½ cups shredded process Swiss
   cheese (6 ounces)

   Paprika or snipped fresh
   parsley (optional)

   Fresh tarragon sprigs
   (optional)

1 Cook lasagna noodles according to package directions; drain. Rinse with cold water; drain again.

2 Meanwhile, for filling, in a medium bowl stir together egg, ricotta cheese, chicken, and the snipped fresh tarragon.

3 To assemble bundles, spread about ⅓ cup of the filling over each lasagna noodle. Starting from a short end, roll up noodles. Place bundles, seam sides down, in a 2-quart rectangular baking dish; set aside.

4 For sauce, in a medium saucepan melt margarine. Stir in flour, mustard, salt, and pepper. Add milk all at once. Cook and stir until thickened and bubbly. Gradually add cheese, stirring until melted after each addition. Pour sauce over lasagna bundles.

5 Cover and bake in a 375°F oven for 30 to 35 minutes or until heated through. Let stand for 10 minutes. Transfer lasagna bundles to dinner plates. Stir sauce in baking dish; spoon the sauce over bundles. If desired, sprinkle with paprika and garnish with fresh tarragon sprigs.

Nutrition Facts per serving: 377 cal., 20 g total fat (10 g sat. fat), 103 mg chol., 501 mg sodium, 23 g carbo., 25 g pro.

buffet CHICKEN SCALLOP

What makes this perfect for a buffet? With both stuffing and juicy chicken, it looks great and tastes absolutely wonderful.

Prep: 30 minutes
Bake: 25 minutes
Oven: 350°F
Stand: 10 minutes
Makes: 12 servings

2 tablespoons butter or margarine

1 large onion, chopped

¾ cup chopped green sweet pepper

3 cups herb-seasoned stuffing mix

1 cup chicken broth

3 eggs, slightly beaten

1 10.75-ounce can condensed cream of celery soup

4 cups chopped cooked chicken or turkey (about 1¼ pounds)

1½ cups cooked rice*

1 10.75-ounce can condensed cream of chicken soup

½ cup dairy sour cream

¼ cup milk

1 Lightly grease a 9x13-inch baking pan or baking dish; set aside. Preheat oven to 350°F. In a large skillet melt butter over medium heat. Add onion and sweet pepper; cook until tender.

2 In large bowl combine stuffing mix and broth; stir in eggs and cream of celery soup. Stir in onion mixture, chicken, and cooked rice. Spread in prepared pan or dish.

3 Bake, uncovered, for 25 to 30 minutes or until an instant-read thermometer inserted in the center registers 160°F. Let stand for 10 minutes before serving.

4 Meanwhile, for sauce, in a small saucepan combine cream of chicken soup, sour cream, and milk; heat and stir until smooth and heated through. Serve sauce with baked chicken mixture.

Nutrition Facts per serving: 286 cal., 12 g total fat (5 g sat. fat), 106 mg chol., 758 mg sodium, 23 g carbo., 19 g pro.

*Test Kitchen Tip: For 1½ cups cooked rice, in a medium saucepan combine 1 cup water and ½ cup uncooked long grain rice. Bring to boiling; reduce heat. Simmer, covered, for 15 to 18 minutes or until rice is tender.

chicken NOODLE CASSEROLE

This version of chicken and noodles bakes the comfort-food classic in a casserole with cheese and sour cream for extra flavor and richness.

Prep: 30 minutes
Bake: 30 minutes
Oven: 350°F
Makes: 4 to 6 servings

- 4 **ounces dried medium noodles (2 cups)**
- 1 **cup sliced fresh mushrooms**
- ½ **cup chopped green or red sweet pepper**
- 3 **tablespoons sliced green onions**
- 2 **tablespoons butter or margarine**
- 2 **cups chopped cooked chicken (about 10 ounces)**
- 1 **10.75-ounce can condensed cream of chicken or cream of broccoli soup**
- 1 **cup loose-pack frozen peas and carrots**
- 1 **cup shredded cheddar cheese (4 ounces)**
- ½ **cup dairy sour cream**
- ⅛ **teaspoon ground black pepper**
- ⅓ **cup fine dry bread crumbs**
- 2 **tablespoons grated Parmesan cheese**
- 2 **tablespoons butter or margarine, melted**

1 Cook noodles according to package directions; drain. Set aside.

2 Meanwhile, in a large saucepan cook mushrooms, sweet pepper, and green onions in 2 tablespoons hot butter until tender. Stir in chicken, cream of chicken soup, peas and carrots, cheddar cheese, sour cream, and black pepper. Bring to boiling over medium heat, stirring frequently. Gently fold in cooked noodles. Spoon into an ungreased 2-quart casserole.

3 In a small bowl combine bread crumbs, Parmesan cheese, and 2 tablespoons melted butter. Sprinkle crumb mixture over chicken mixture.

4 Bake, uncovered, in a 350°F oven for 30 to 35 minutes or until heated through and top is golden.

Nutrition Facts per serving: 659 cal., 40 g total fat (20 g sat. fat), 170 mg chol., 1,229 mg sodium, 38 g carbo., 38 g pro.

tex-mex CHICKEN AND RICE CASSEROLE

Prep: 20 minutes
Bake: 25 minutes
Stand: 5 minutes
Oven: 425°F
Makes: 6 servings

½ **cup chopped onion (1 medium)**

1 **tablespoon olive oil**

1 **6.9-ounce package chicken-flavor rice and vermicelli mix**

1 **14-ounce can chicken broth**

2 **cups water**

2 **cups chopped cooked chicken**

1 **cup chopped seeded tomatoes (2 medium)**

3 **tablespoons canned diced green chile peppers, drained**

1 **teaspoon dried basil, crushed**

1½ **teaspoons chili powder**

⅛ **teaspoon ground cumin**

⅛ **teaspoon ground black pepper**

½ **cup shredded cheddar cheese (2 ounces)**

1 In a medium saucepan cook onion in hot oil over medium heat until tender. Stir in rice and vermicelli mix (including seasoning package); cook and stir for 2 minutes. Stir in broth and water. Bring to boiling; reduce heat. Cover and simmer for 20 minutes (liquid will not be fully absorbed).

2 Transfer the rice mixture to a large bowl. Stir in chicken, tomatoes, chile peppers, basil, chili powder, cumin, and black pepper. Transfer to a 2-quart casserole.

3 Bake, covered, in a 425°F oven for 25 minutes. Sprinkle with cheese. Let stand for 5 minutes before serving.

Nutrition Facts per serving: 280 cal., 10 g total fat (4 g sat. fat), 52 mg chol., 931 mg sodium, 28 g carbo., 20 g pro.

Make Ahead: Prepare as above through Step 1. Cover and chill for up to 24 hours. Bake, covered, in a 425°F oven about 40 minutes or until heated through. Uncover and sprinkle with cheese. Let stand for 5 minutes before serving.

three-cheese ziti AND
SMOKED CHICKEN CASSEROLE

Prep: 25 minutes
Bake: 25 minutes
Stand: 10 minutes
Oven: 375°F
Makes: 6 servings

Butter

12 ounces dried cut ziti

3 tablespoons butter or
   margarine

2 cloves garlic, minced

3 tablespoons all-purpose flour

¼ teaspoon salt

¼ teaspoon ground white
   pepper

3½ cups milk

8 ounces Asiago cheese, finely
   shredded (1½ cups)

4 ounces fontina cheese, finely
   shredded (1 cup)

2 ounces blue cheese, crumbled
   (½ cup)

2 cups chopped smoked chicken
   or shredded purchased
   roasted chicken

⅓ cup panko (Japanese-style)
   bread crumbs or fine dry
   bread crumbs

2 teaspoons white truffle oil or
   melted butter

1 Preheat oven to 375°F. Butter a 2-quart baking dish; set aside. Cook pasta according to package directions. Drain pasta; return to hot saucepan. Cover and keep warm.

2 Meanwhile, in a medium saucepan melt the 3 tablespoons butter over medium heat. Add garlic; cook for 30 seconds. Stir in flour, salt, and white pepper. Add milk all at once. Cook and stir until thickened and bubbly. Add Asiago, fontina, and blue cheeses, stirring until melted. Add chicken, stirring to combine.

3 Pour cheese mixture over cooked ziti; gently toss to coat. Transfer mixture to the prepared baking dish. In a small bowl combine panko crumbs and truffle oil. Sprinkle crumb mixture evenly over mixture in baking dish.

4 Bake about 25 minutes or until bubbly and lightly browned. Let stand for 10 minutes before serving.

Nutrition Facts per serving: 753 cal., 39 g total fat (22 g sat. fat), 141 mg chol., 953 mg sodium, 56 g carbo., 43 g pro.

herb-roasted CHICKEN

Prep: 20 minutes
Roast: 75 minutes
Stand: 10 minutes
Oven: 375°F
Makes: 4 servings

1   3½ to 4-pound whole broiler chicken

2   tablespoons butter or margarine, melted

2   cloves garlic, minced

1   teaspoon dried basil, crushed

½   teaspoon ground sage

½   teaspoon dried thyme, crushed

¼   teaspoon salt

¼   teaspoon lemon-pepper seasoning or ground black pepper

1 Preheat oven to 375°F. Rinse the inside of chicken; pat dry with paper towels. Skewer neck skin of chicken to back; tie legs to tail. Twist wing tips under back. Place chicken, breast side up, on a rack in a shallow roasting pan. Brush with melted butter; rub garlic over chicken.

2 In a small bowl stir together basil, sage, thyme, salt, and lemon-pepper seasoning; rub onto chicken. If desired, insert a meat thermometer into center of an inside thigh muscle. (The thermometer should not touch bone.)

3 Roast, uncovered, for 75 to 90 minutes or until drumsticks move easily in their sockets and chicken is no longer pink (180°F). Remove chicken from oven. Cover; let stand for 10 minutes before carving.

Nutrition Facts per serving: 625 cal., 45 g total fat (14 g sat. fat), 217 mg chol., 408 mg sodium, 1 g carbo., 50 g pro.

roast chicken
SOUTHWESTERN-STYLE

Squares of freshly baked corn bread add just the right touch to this easy-to-make roasted chicken.

Prep: 50 minutes
Roast: 1 hour 45 minutes
Oven: 325°F
Stand: 10 minutes
Makes: 10 servings

1 **5- to 6-pound whole roasting chicken**

1 **tablespoon olive oil or cooking oil**

1 **teaspoon dried oregano, crushed**

½ **teaspoon ground cumin**

1 **lime, cut into 6 wedges**

2 **cilantro sprigs**

1 **15-ounce can black beans, rinsed and drained**

1 **small tomato, chopped**

1 **small cucumber, seeded and chopped**

¼ **cup chopped green onion**

2 **tablespoons snipped cilantro or parsley**

1 **teaspoon finely shredded lime peel**

2 **tablespoons lime juice**

1 **tablespoon olive oil or cooking oil**

1 **clove garlic, minced**

¼ **teaspoon salt**

Cilantro sprigs (optional)

Lime wedges (optional)

1 Brush chicken with 1 tablespoon oil. In a small bowl combine oregano and cumin; sprinkle over the outside of the bird, then rub into skin. Place 6 lime wedges and 2 cilantro sprigs in body cavity. Tuck the drumsticks under the band of skin that crosses the tail. If there is no band, tie drumsticks to the tail. Twist the wing tips under the chicken.

2 Place chicken, breast side up, on a rack in a shallow pan. Insert a meat thermometer into the center of one of the thigh muscles. The bulb should not touch the bone. Roast, uncovered, in a 325°F oven for 1¾ to 2½ hours or until meat thermometer registers 180°F. At this time, chicken is no longer pink and the drumsticks move easily in their sockets. When the bird is two-thirds done, cut the band of skin or string between the drumsticks so the thighs cook more evenly.

3 Meanwhile, for black bean salsa, in a bowl combine black beans, tomato, cucumber, green onion, cilantro, lime peel, lime juice, 1 tablespoon oil, garlic, and salt. Mix well. Cover and chill until serving time.

4 Remove chicken from oven and cover it with foil. Let chicken stand for 10 to 20 minutes before carving. Serve black bean salsa with chicken. Garnish with additional cilantro and lime wedges, if desired.

Nutrition Facts per serving: 310 cal., 16 g total fat (4 g sat. fat), 93 mg chol., 214 mg sodium, 9 g carbo., 35 g pro.

Make Ahead: Prepare salsa; cover and chill up to 12 hours.

fruit-stuffed ROASTED CHICKEN

Roast: 1¾ hours
Oven: 325°F
Makes: 10 servings

1 **5- to 6-pound whole roasting chicken**

Salt and ground black pepper

¼ **cup margarine or butter, melted**

¼ **cup dry sherry**

4½ **teaspoons snipped fresh thyme or 1½ teaspoons dried thyme, crushed**

2 **teaspoons finely shredded orange peel**

2 **medium apples, cored and chopped (2 cups)**

1 **medium onion, chopped (½ cup)**

½ **cup chopped celery**

2 **cups cubed French bread (¾-inch cubes)**

10 **pitted prunes or dried apricots, cut up**

1 **cup seedless green grapes, halved**

2 **tablespoons orange juice**

1 Rinse chicken; pat dry. Sprinkle body cavity with salt and pepper. In a small bowl combine 2 tablespoons melted margarine, 2 tablespoons sherry, 1 tablespoon fresh thyme or 1 teaspoon dried thyme, and 1 teaspoon orange peel. Brush chicken with sherry mixture.

2 For stuffing, in a medium skillet cook apples, onion, and celery in the remaining melted margarine about 5 minutes or until tender. In a large bowl combine apple mixture, French bread, prunes, grapes, orange juice, remaining dry sherry, remaining fresh thyme, and remaining orange peel. (Stuffing will become more moist while cooking.) Spoon some of the stuffing loosely into the neck cavity. Pull neck skin to back; fasten with a small skewer. Lightly spoon the remaining stuffing into the body cavity. Tuck drumsticks under the band of skin that crosses the tail. If there is no band, tie drumsticks to the tail. Twist the wing tips under the chicken.

3 Place stuffed chicken, breast side up, on a rack in a shallow roasting pan. Insert a meat thermometer into the center of an inside thigh muscle. The bulb should not touch the bone. Roast, uncovered, in a 325°F oven for 1¾ to 2½ hours or until meat thermometer registers 180°F to 185°F. At this time, chicken is no longer pink and the drumsticks move easily in their sockets. When the bird is two-thirds done, cut the band of skin or string between the drumsticks so the thighs will cook evenly.

4 Remove from oven; cover with foil. Let stand for 10 to 20 minutes before carving.

Nutrition Facts per serving: 393 cal., 18 g total fat (5 g sat. fat), 93 mg chol., 250 mg sodium, 22 g carbo., 33 g pro.

roasted chicken WITH
CITRUS SALSA

Prep: 25 minutes
Roast: 1¼ hours
Stand: 15 minutes
Oven: 375°F
Makes: 6 servings

- 1 **3-pound whole broiler-fryer chicken**
- 1 **tablespoon cooking oil**
- 2 **cloves garlic, minced**
- 2 **teaspoons ground cinnamon**
- ½ **teaspoon salt**
- ½ **teaspoon ground nutmeg**
- ¼ **teaspoon black pepper**
- 3 **tablespoons honey**
- ⅓ **cup dried tart red cherries**
- 1⅓ **cups orange sections, halved (about 4 oranges)**
- 2 **nectarines, pitted and chopped**
- 2 **tablespoons snipped fresh cilantro**
- 1 **fresh jalapeño chile pepper, seeded and chopped***
- 1 **tablespoon lime juice**
  Fresh cilantro sprigs (optional)

1 Remove skin from chicken (except for wings). Tie legs to tail. Twist wing tips under back. Place chicken, breast side up, on a rack in a roasting pan. In a bowl combine oil and garlic; brush onto chicken. In another bowl combine cinnamon, salt, nutmeg, and black pepper. Sprinkle evenly over chicken. Insert an oven-going meat thermometer into center of an inside thigh muscle.

2 Roast chicken, uncovered, in a 375°F oven for 1 hour. Remove string from legs. Brush honey over chicken. Roast about 15 minutes more or until drumsticks move easily in their sockets, chicken is no longer pink, and meat thermometer registers 180°F. Remove chicken from oven. Cover; let stand for 15 minutes.

3 Meanwhile, for salsa, place cherries in a small saucepan; cover with water. Bring to boiling; remove from heat. Cover and let stand 5 minutes. Drain well. In a medium bowl combine drained cherries, orange sections, nectarines, snipped cilantro, jalapeño pepper, and lime juice. Cover and chill until ready to serve. Serve with chicken. If desired, garnish with cilantro sprigs.

Nutrition Facts per serving: 250 cal., 6 g total fat (1 g sat. fat), 76 mg chol., 262 mg sodium, 26 g carbo., 25 g pro.

*Note: Because chile peppers contain volatile oils that can burn your skin and eyes, avoid direct contact with them as much as possible. When working with chile peppers, wear plastic or rubber gloves. If your bare hands do touch the peppers, wash your hands and nails well with soap and warm water.

roasted TARRAGON CHICKEN

Prep: 15 minutes
Roast: 45 minutes
Oven: 375°F
Makes: 6 servings

3 tablespoons olive oil

2½ teaspoons dried tarragon, crushed

2 cloves garlic, minced

½ teaspoon coarsely ground black pepper

¼ teaspoon salt

1 pound red and/or yellow cherry tomatoes

8 shallots

2½ to 3 pounds meaty chicken pieces (breast halves, thighs, and drumsticks), skinned

Fresh tarragon sprigs (optional)

1 Preheat oven to 375°F. In a medium bowl stir together olive oil, dried tarragon, garlic, pepper, and salt. Add cherry tomatoes and shallots; toss gently to coat. Use a slotted spoon to transfer tomatoes and shallots to another bowl, reserving the olive oil mixture.

2 Place chicken in a shallow roasting pan. Brush chicken with the reserved olive oil mixture.

3 Roast chicken for 20 minutes. Add shallots; roast for 15 minutes more. Add tomatoes; roast for 10 to 12 minutes more or until chicken is no longer pink (170°F for breasts; 180°F for thighs and drumsticks) and vegetables are tender. If desired, garnish with fresh tarragon.

Nutrition Facts per serving: 253 cal., 13 g total fat (3 g sat. fat), 77 mg chol., 173 mg sodium, 8 g carbo., 26 g pro.

roasted ITALIAN CHICKEN

Prep: 15 minutes
Roast: 1¼ hours
Oven: 375°F
Makes: 6 servings

2 tablespoons balsamic vinegar

2 tablespoons olive oil

1 tablespoon lemon juice

3 cloves garlic, minced

½ teaspoon salt

½ teaspoon coarsely ground
  black pepper

1 tablespoon snipped fresh
  oregano or 1 teaspoon dried
  oregano, crushed

1 tablespoon snipped fresh
  basil or 1 teaspoon dried
  basil, crushed

1½ teaspoons snipped fresh
  thyme or ½ teaspoon thyme,
  crushed

1 3- to 3½-pound whole broiler-
  fryer chicken

1 In a small bowl whisk together vinegar, oil, lemon juice, garlic, salt, pepper, oregano, basil, and thyme. Set aside.

2 Place chicken, breast side up, on a rack in a shallow roasting pan. Tie legs to tail. Twist wing tips under back. Slip your fingers between the skin and the breast and leg meat of the chicken, forming a pocket. Spoon herb mixture into pocket.

3 Roast, uncovered, in a 375°F oven for 1¼ to 1½ hours or until drumsticks move easily in their sockets, chicken is no longer pink, and a meat thermometer inserted into inside thigh muscle registers 180°F. Remove chicken from oven. Cover with foil; let stand for 10 minutes before carving.

Nutrition Facts per serving: 266 cal., 17 g total fat (4 g sat. fat), 79 mg chol., 268 mg sodium, 2 g carbo., 25 g pro.

roasted CRANBERRY CHICKEN

Prep: 25 minutes
Bake: 20 minutes
Oven: 375°F
Makes: 4 servings

8   **small chicken thighs (2 to 2¼ pounds), skinned**

¾   **cup low-calorie cranberry juice**

¾   **cup fresh cranberries**

2   **sprigs fresh thyme**

4   **teaspoons packed brown sugar**

  Salt and ground black pepper

  Fresh thyme leaves

1 Preheat oven to 375°F. Coat extra-large ovenproof skillet with nonstick cooking spray. Heat over medium-high heat. Sprinkle ¼ teaspoon each salt and pepper on chicken. In hot skillet cook, meaty sides down, 5 minutes, turning once, until well-browned on both sides. Transfer skillet to oven. Roast, uncovered, 20 minutes, until chicken is no longer pink (180°F).

2 Meanwhile, in saucepan combine cranberry juice, cranberries, thyme sprigs, brown sugar, and ¼ teaspoon salt. Bring to boiling. Simmer, uncovered, 15 to 20 minutes, until slightly thickened. Discard thyme sprigs. Serve chicken with sauce. Sprinkle with thyme leaves.

Nutrition Facts per serving: 187 cal., 5 g total fat (1 g sat. fat), 107 mg chol., 383 mg sodium, 9 g carbo., 26 g pro.

skillets
AND STIR-FRIES

Italian Chicken, *recipe page 140*

chicken WITH SKILLET TOMATO SAUCE

Rigatoni, a deftly seasoned tomato sauce, almonds, and olives all make this chicken dish a winner.

Start to Finish: 1 hour
10 minutes

Makes: 4 servings

- 2 **to 2½ pounds meaty chicken pieces (breasts, thighs, and drumsticks)**
- ¼ **teaspoon salt**
- ¼ **teaspoon pepper**
- ¼ **cup slivered almonds**
- 2 **tablespoons olive oil**
- 6 **ounces packaged dried rigatoni**
- ½ **cup sliced onion**
- 3 **cloves garlic, minced**
- 4 **medium tomatoes, seeded and cut up (1½ pounds)**
- ¼ **cup tomato paste**
- 1 **tablespoon red wine vinegar**
- ½ **teaspoon sugar**
- ¼ **teaspoon salt**
- ⅛ **teaspoon crushed red pepper**
- ¼ **cup coarsely chopped, pimiento-stuffed green olives**
  Fresh marjoram sprigs (optional)

1 Skin chicken, if desired. Sprinkle with the first ¼ teaspoon salt and pepper; set aside. Place almonds in a 12-inch skillet. Cook over medium heat for 5 to 7 minutes or until almonds are lightly toasted, stirring often; remove from pan and set aside.

2 In the same 12-inch skillet heat olive oil. Add chicken to the skillet, placing meaty pieces toward the center. Cook, uncovered, over medium heat for 15 minutes or until lightly browned, turning to brown evenly. Reduce heat. Cook, covered, for 30 to 35 minutes or until chicken is tender and no longer pink.

3 Meanwhile, cook pasta according to package directions; drain and keep warm. Remove chicken from skillet; drain off all but 2 tablespoons drippings. Cover chicken and keep warm while preparing sauce.

4 For sauce, cook onion and garlic in the reserved drippings until tender; transfer to a blender container or food processor bowl. Add the tomatoes, tomato paste, vinegar, sugar, ¼ teaspoon salt, and red pepper. Cover and blend or process until nearly smooth. Return mixture to skillet. Stir in olives. Bring to boiling; reduce heat. Boil gently, uncovered, about 10 minutes or until desired consistency.

5 Divide pasta among four bowls or plates. Top with a piece of chicken. Spoon sauce over chicken and pasta. Sprinkle with toasted almonds. Garnish with marjoram sprigs, if desired.

Nutrition Facts per serving: 599 cal., 27 g total fat (5 g sat. fat), 104 mg chol., 426 mg sodium, 49 g carbo., 43 g pro.

maryland fried chicken WITH CREAMY GRAVY

What sets this fried chicken apart from the typical recipe is that milk is added after partially cooking the chicken so the pieces simmer rather than fry.

Prep: 20 minutes
Cook: 55 minutes
Makes: 6 servings

- 1 egg, beaten
- 3 tablespoons milk
- 1 cup finely crushed saltine crackers (28 crackers)
- 1 teaspoon dried thyme, crushed
- ½ teaspoon paprika
- ⅛ teaspoon black pepper
- 2½ to 3 pounds meaty chicken pieces (breasts, thighs, and drumsticks)
- 2 to 3 tablespoons cooking oil
- 1 cup milk
  Creamy Gravy*

① In a small bowl combine egg and the 3 tablespoons milk. In a shallow bowl combine crushed crackers, thyme, paprika, and pepper. Dip chicken pieces, one at a time, in egg mixture; roll in cracker mixture.

② In a large skillet brown chicken in hot oil over medium heat for 10 to 15 minutes, turning occasionally. Drain well.

③ Add the 1 cup milk to skillet. Heat just to boiling. Reduce heat to medium-low; cover tightly. Cook for 35 minutes. Uncover; cook about 10 minutes more or until chicken is no longer pink (170°F for breasts; 180°F for thighs and drumsticks). Transfer chicken to a serving platter, reserving drippings for gravy. Cover chicken and keep warm. Prepare Creamy Gravy. If desired, serve with mashed potatoes.

*Creamy Gravy: Skim fat from drippings. Reserve 3 tablespoons of the drippings in skillet. In a screw-top jar combine ¾ cup milk, 3 tablespoons all-purpose flour, ¼ teaspoon salt, and ⅛ teaspoon black pepper; cover and shake until well combined. Add to skillet. Stir in an additional 1 cup milk. Cook over medium heat, stirring constantly, until thickened and bubbly. Cook and stir for 1 minute more. (If desired, thin with additional milk.) Makes about 1¾ cups.

Nutrition Facts per serving: 404 cal., 20 g total fat (5 g sat. fat), 131 mg chol., 423 mg sodium, 19 g carbo., 35 g pro.

green chile FRIED CHICKEN

Fried chicken lovers will ask for this sour cream-and-chile pepper seasoned dish time and again. Adjust the heat level by adding more or less bottled hot pepper sauce. It's a satisfying meal when served with baked beans and potato salad.

Makes: 4 to 6 servings

1 8-ounce carton dairy sour cream

¼ cup milk

1 4-ounce can diced green chile peppers

2 tablespoons snipped fresh cilantro

2 tablespoons lime juice

1 clove garlic, minced

¾ teaspoon ground cumin

½ teaspoon salt

¼ teaspoon ground black pepper

1 2.5- to 3-pound cut up broiler-fryer chicken, skinned, if desired

¾ cup all-purpose flour

Cooking oil

Bottled hot pepper sauce (optional)

Lime wedges (optional)

1 For marinade, in a medium bowl combine sour cream, milk, chile peppers, cilantro, lime juice, garlic, cumin, salt, and black pepper. Place chicken pieces in a resealable plastic bag set in a shallow dish. Pour sour cream mixture over chicken; seal bag. Refrigerate for 8 to 24 hours, turning bag occasionally.

2 Place flour in a shallow dish. Remove chicken from bag; discard marinade. Add chicken pieces to flour, a few at a time, turning to coat.

3 Add oil to a 12-inch heavy skillet to a depth of ¼ to ½ inch. Heat over medium-high heat until hot (350°F). Reduce heat. Carefully add chicken to the skillet. Cook, uncovered, over medium heat about 40 minutes or until chicken is no longer pink (170°F for breasts; 180°F for thighs and drumsticks), turning occasionally to brown evenly. Drain on paper towels. If desired, serve with bottled hot pepper sauce and lime wedges.

Nutrition Facts per serving: 608 cal., 42 g total fat (14 g sat. fat), 125 mg chol., 501 mg sodium, 22 g carbo., 36 g pro.

chicken PICCATA

Start to Finish: 20 minutes
Makes: 4 servings

4   small skinless, boneless
   chicken breast halves
   (about 1½ pounds)

1   tablespoon Dijon-style
   mustard

   Salt

   Black pepper

¼   cup seasoned fine dry bread
   crumbs

¼   cup olive oil

2   small lemons

8   ounces haricot verts, trimmed
   if desired, or green beans,
   trimmed and halved
   lengthwise

1   tablespoon capers

   Hot buttered pasta (optional)

1 Place a chicken breast half between two sheets of plastic wrap. Lightly pound using the flat side of a meat mallet to an even thickness. Repeat with remaining chicken breast halves. Brush chicken lightly with mustard; sprinkle with salt and pepper. Place chicken on a waxed paper lined baking sheet. Sprinkle chicken with crumbs to coat.

2 Heat 2 tablespoons of the oil in a very large skillet on medium to medium-high heat; add chicken breast halves and cook 4 minutes per side or until no pink remains.

3 Meanwhile, slice one of the lemons. Transfer chicken to serving plates. Add remaining oil to skillet. Cook beans in hot oil 4 to 5 minutes or until beans are crisp tender, adding the lemon slices the last minute of cooking. Remove to plates with slotted spoon. Juice remaining lemon and add lemon juice and capers to skillet; cook 30 seconds. Drizzle on chicken and beans. Serve with pasta, if desired.

Nutrition Facts per serving: 362 cal., 16 g total fat (3 g sat. fat), 99 mg chol., 546 mg sodium, 13 g carbo., 42 g pro.

italian CHICKEN

This dish contains all the best ingredients Italy has to offer—black olives, capers, garlic, basil, wine, olive oil, and tomatoes.

Start to Finish: 40 minutes
Makes: 4 servings

4 skinless, boneless chicken breast halves (about 1 pound total)

2 tablespoons olive oil

1 large onion, halved and thinly sliced

2 cloves garlic, minced

3 large tomatoes, coarsely chopped

¼ cup Greek black olives or ripe olives, pitted and sliced

1 tablespoon capers, drained

¼ teaspoon salt

⅛ teaspoon pepper

¼ cup dry red wine or reduced-sodium chicken broth

2 teaspoons cornstarch

¼ cup snipped fresh basil

2 cups hot cooked couscous

1 Rinse chicken; pat dry. In a large skillet heat 1 tablespoon of the olive oil over medium-high heat. Add chicken; cook for 4 to 5 minutes on each side or until chicken is tender and no longer pink. Remove from pan and keep warm.

2 For sauce, add the remaining olive oil, onion, and garlic to hot skillet. Cook and stir for 2 minutes. Add the tomatoes, olives, capers, salt, and pepper to skillet. Bring to boiling; reduce heat. Simmer, covered, for 3 minutes. Stir together the wine and cornstarch; add to the skillet. Cook and stir until thickened and bubbly. Cook and stir for 2 minutes more. Stir in basil. Pour sauce over chicken. Serve with couscous.

Nutrition Facts per serving: 319 cal., 8 g total fat (2 g sat. fat), 59 mg chol., 289 mg sodium, 32 g carbo., 27 g pro.

pesto chicken breasts WITH
SUMMER SQUASH

Purchased pesto makes preparation easy in this five-ingredient dish.

Start to Finish: 20 minutes
Makes: 4 servings

4 **medium skinless, boneless chicken breast halves (about ¾ pound total)**

1 **tablespoon olive oil**

2 **cups finely chopped zucchini and/or yellow summer squash**

2 **tablespoons homemade or purchased pesto**

2 **tablespoons finely shredded Asiago or Parmesan cheese**

1 In a large nonstick skillet cook chicken in hot oil over medium heat for 4 minutes.

2 Turn chicken; add zucchini and/or squash. Cook for 4 to 6 minutes more or until the chicken is tender and no longer pink (170°F) and squash is crisp-tender, stirring squash gently once or twice. Transfer chicken and squash to four dinner plates. Spread pesto over chicken; sprinkle with Asiago cheese.

Nutrition Facts per serving: 186 cal., 10 g total fat (2 g sat. fat), 55 mg chol., 129 mg sodium, 2 g carbo., 23 g pro.

chicken AND LEMON-BROCCOLI ALFREDO

Jazz up the flavor of purchased alfredo sauce with lemon peel and pepper for this chicken and mushroom skillet dinner.

Start to Finish: 20 minutes
Makes: 4 servings

4 **small skinless, boneless chicken breast halves**

Salt and ground black pepper

8 **ounces mushrooms, halved**

1 **tablespoon olive or cooking oil**

1 **lemon**

3 **cups fresh broccoli florets**

1 **10-ounce container refrigerated light Alfredo pasta sauce**

1 Season chicken with salt and pepper. In a large skillet cook chicken and mushrooms in hot oil for 4 minutes, turning chicken halfway through.

2 Meanwhile, shred 2 teaspoons lemon peel; set aside. Slice lemon. Add broccoli and lemon slices to skillet. Cook, covered, for 8 minutes or until chicken is done (170°F).

3 Place chicken and vegetables on plates. Add Alfredo sauce to skillet; heat through. Add lemon peel and pepper. Serve with chicken.

Nutrition Facts per serving: 295 cal., 12 g total fat (5 g sat. fat), 91 mg chol., 705 mg sodium, 16 g carbo., 35 g pro.

rosemary chicken WITH VEGETABLES

Apple juice and rosemary add both sweet and savory flavors to the sauce for this dish.

Start to Finish: 27 minutes
Makes: 4 servings

- 4 **medium skinless, boneless chicken breast halves**
- ½ **teaspoon lemon-pepper seasoning**
- 2 **tablespoons olive oil**
- 4 **ounces refrigerated spinach or plain linguine**
- 1 **teaspoon bottled minced garlic**
- 2 **medium zucchini and/or yellow summer squash, sliced ¼ inch thick (2½ cups)**
- ½ **cup apple juice**
- 2 **teaspoons snipped fresh rosemary or ½ teaspoon dried rosemary, crushed**
- 2 **tablespoons dry white wine or chicken broth**
- 2 **teaspoons cornstarch**
- 1 **cup halved cherry or grape tomatoes**

  Fresh rosemary sprigs (optional)

1 Sprinkle chicken with lemon-pepper seasoning. In a large skillet cook chicken in hot oil over medium heat for 8 to 10 minutes or until chicken is no longer pink, turning once. Transfer chicken to a platter; cover and keep warm. Meanwhile, cook pasta according to package directions; drain and keep warm.

2 Add garlic to skillet; cook for 15 seconds. Add zucchini, apple juice, and rosemary. Bring to boiling; reduce heat. Cover and simmer for 2 minutes.

3 In a small bowl stir together wine and cornstarch; add to skillet. Cook and stir until thickened and bubbly; cook for 2 minutes more. Stir in tomatoes. Serve vegetables and pasta with chicken. If desired, garnish with rosemary sprigs.

Nutrition Facts per serving: 326 cal., 10 g total fat (2 g sat. fat), 95 mg chol., 247 mg sodium, 25 g carbo., 33 g pro.

southwest CHICKEN SKILLET

Chicken, sweet peppers, zucchini, black beans, and corn—flavored with fajita seasoning—create this quick skillet dinner.

Start to Finish: 30 minutes
Makes: 4 servings

- 1 **1- to 1.5-ounce envelope fajita seasoning mix**
- ½ **cup water**
- 2 **tablespoons cooking oil**
- 12 **ounces skinless, boneless chicken breast halves, cut into 1-inch pieces**
   Nonstick spray coating
- 1 **medium yellow or green sweet pepper, cut into squares**
- 1 **small zucchini, bias-sliced**
- ½ **small onion, cut into thin wedges**
- ⅔ **cup salsa**
- 1 **teaspoon chili powder**
- ½ **cup frozen whole kernel corn**
- ½ **cup cooked or canned black beans, rinsed and drained**
- 8 **8-inch flour tortillas (optional)**
- ½ **cup shredded reduced-fat Colby-Monterey Jack cheese (optional)**

1 For marinade, in a medium bowl combine fajita mix, water, and oil. Add chicken to marinade. Stir to coat. Let stand at room temperature for 15 minutes.

2 Spray a large skillet with nonstick coating. Preheat over medium heat. Add sweet pepper, zucchini, and onion; cook and stir for 2 to 3 minutes or until crisp-tender. Remove from skillet.

3 Drain chicken; discard marinade. Add chicken to skillet. (If necessary, add 1 tablespoon cooking oil during cooking.) Cook and stir for 4 to 5 minutes or until no pink remains. Return vegetables to skillet. Stir together salsa and chili powder. Add salsa mixture, corn, and beans to skillet. Cook and stir for 1 to 2 minutes more or until heated through. Serve with warm tortillas and cheese, if desired. (To heat tortillas, wrap in microwave-safe paper towels; microwave on high power for 30 seconds).

Nutrition Facts per serving: 191 cal., 6 g total fat (1 g sat. fat), 45 mg chol., 298 mg sodium, 18 g carbo., 20 g pro.

skillet CHICKEN CAESAR

Prep: 5 minutes
Microwave: 6 to 8 minutes
Cook: 15 minutes
Makes: 4 servings

- 4 **boneless skinless chicken breast halves (5 ounces each)**
- 1 **bottle (8 ounces) reduced-fat creamy Caesar dressing**
- 1 **tablespoon extra virgin olive oil**
- 2 **sweet red peppers, seeded and cut into ¼-inch strips**
- 1 **cup heavy cream**
- ½ **package (22 ounces) frozen mashed potatoes**
- ¼ **teaspoon salt**

1 Place chicken breasts in large resealable plastic bag; add 2 tablespoons of the dressing. Seal and marinate at room temperature for 15 minutes.

2 In a large sauté pan heat oil over medium-high heat. Add peppers and cook 5 minutes or until peppers are softened. Remove and reserve.

3 Stir together 3 tablespoons of the dressing, ¼ cup of the cream, and enough water to make 1½ cups. Place mashed potatoes (2⅔ cups) in microwave-safe bowl; stir in dressing mixture. Microwave on high 6 to 8 minutes, stirring once. Cover until ready to serve.

4 Meanwhile, remove chicken from bag. Add to pan; sprinkle with salt. Sauté 4 minutes on one side. Turn and cook another 4 minutes, or until browned. Reduce heat to medium-low. Add peppers back to skillet along with remaining dressing and cream.

5 Cook another 2 minutes or until chicken is cooked through and registers 160°F on an instant-read thermometer. Stir mashed potatoes and reheat if necessary; serve with chicken and peppers.

Nutrition Facts per serving: 679 cal., 37 g total fat (17 g sat. fat), 220 mg chol., 835 mg sodium, 36 g carbo., 48 g pro.

feta-stuffed CHICKEN

Start to Finish: 30 minutes
Makes: 4 servings

¼ cup crumbled basil-and-
tomato feta cheese
(1 ounce)*

2 tablespoons fat-free cream
cheese (1 ounce)

4 skinless, boneless chicken
breast halves (about
1¼ pounds total)

¼ to ½ teaspoon black pepper
Dash salt

1 teaspoon olive oil or cooking
oil

¼ cup chicken broth

1 10-ounce package prewashed
fresh spinach, trimmed
(8 cups)

2 tablespoons walnut or pecan
pieces, toasted

1 tablespoon lemon juice
Lemon slices, halved
(optional)

1 In a small bowl combine feta cheese and cream cheese; set aside. Using a sharp knife, cut a horizontal slit through the thickest portion of each chicken breast half to form a pocket. Stuff pockets with the cheese mixture. If necessary, secure openings with wooden toothpicks. Sprinkle chicken with pepper and salt.

2 In a large nonstick skillet cook chicken in hot oil over medium-high heat about 12 minutes or until tender and no longer pink, turning once (reduce heat to medium if chicken browns too quickly). Remove chicken from skillet. Cover and keep warm.

3 Carefully add chicken broth to skillet. Bring to boiling; add half of the spinach. Cover and cook about 3 minutes or just until spinach is wilted. Remove spinach from skillet, reserving liquid in pan. Repeat with remaining spinach. Return all spinach to skillet. Stir in the nuts and lemon juice.

4 To serve, divide spinach mixture among four dinner plates. Top with chicken breasts. If desired, garnish with lemon slices.

Nutrition Facts per serving: 231 cal., 8 g total fat (2 g sat. fat), 90 mg chol., 334 mg sodium, 2 g carbo., 38 g pro.

*Note: If basil-and-tomato feta cheese is not available, stir 1 teaspoon finely snipped fresh basil and 1 teaspoon snipped oil-pack dried tomatoes, drained, into ¼ cup plain feta cheese.

chicken WITH RED AND YELLOW CHERRY TOMATOES

A simple topping of delightfully tangy red and yellow cherry tomatoes makes this meal the perfect weeknight fare.

Prep: 15 minutes
Cook: 10 minutes
Makes: 4 servings

4 skinless, boneless chicken breast halves (1 to 1¼ pounds total)
½ teaspoon kosher salt
¼ teaspoon freshly ground black pepper
2 teaspoons extra-virgin olive oil
2 cups red and yellow cherry tomatoes, halved
2 tablespoons water
2 tablespoons chopped fresh flat-leaf parsley or basil or 1 tablespoon chopped fresh tarragon
1 tablespoon white wine vinegar

1 Sprinkle chicken with ¼ teaspoon of the kosher salt and ⅛ teaspoon of the pepper. In a large nonstick skillet heat olive oil over medium-high heat. Add chicken; cook for 10 to 12 minutes or until chicken is no longer pink (170°F), turning once. Transfer chicken to a serving platter; cover and keep warm.

2 Drain fat from skillet. Add tomatoes, the water, parsley, vinegar, the remaining ¼ teaspoon salt, and the remaining ⅛ teaspoon pepper to skillet. Bring to boiling; reduce heat. Simmer, uncovered, for 3 to 4 minutes or until tomatoes begin to soften, stirring occasionally. Serve the tomato mixture over chicken.

Nutrition Facts per serving: 163 cal., 4 g total fat (1 g sat. fat), 66 mg chol., 321 mg sodium, 4 g carbo., 27 g pro.

sweet-and-sour CHICKEN WITH RICE NOODLES

Rice noodles are a terrific timesaver because they need no cooking. Just let them stand in warm water about 15 minutes to rehydrate. You can use them as you would pasta or rice with a saucy mixture on top or plain.

Start to Finish: 30 minutes
Makes: 4 servings

- 6 **ounces rice noodles or 2 cups hot cooked rice**
- 1 **8-ounce can pineapple chunks (juice pack)**
- ¾ **cup chicken broth**
- ¼ **cup vinegar**
- 3 **tablespoons brown sugar**
- 2 **tablespoons cornstarch**
- 2 **tablespoons soy sauce**
- 1 **tablespoon cooking oil**
- ½ **teaspoon bottled minced garlic or 1 clove garlic, minced**
- 1 **cup sliced celery**
- 1 **medium onion, cut into thin wedges**
- 1 **small red or green sweet pepper, cut into thin bite-size strips**
- 12 **ounces skinless, boneless chicken breasts, cut into bite-size strips**

1 Break rice noodles, if using, into a large bowl; cover with warm water. Let stand for 15 minutes while preparing chicken mixture.

2 Drain pineapple, reserving juice (you should have about ⅓ cup). For sauce, in a small bowl stir together the reserved pineapple juice, the chicken broth, vinegar, brown sugar, cornstarch, and soy sauce. Set aside.

3 Heat the oil in a wok or large skillet over medium-high heat. (Add more oil as necessary during cooking.) Stir-fry garlic in hot oil for 15 seconds. Add celery and onion; stir-fry for 2 minutes. Add the sweet pepper; stir-fry for 2 minutes more. Remove vegetables from wok.

4 Add the chicken to the hot wok. Stir-fry for 2 to 3 minutes or until no longer pink. Stir sauce; add to wok. Cook and stir until thickened and bubbly. Add cooked vegetables and pineapple. Cook and stir for 2 minutes more or until heated through. Drain rice noodles, if using; arrange noodles or hot cooked rice on four dinner plates. Top with chicken mixture.

Nutrition Facts per serving: 388 cal., 6 g total fat (1 g sat. fat), 45 mg chol., 706 mg sodium, 64 g carbo., 19 g pro.

garlic-chicken STIR-FRY

Start to Finish: 25 minutes
Makes: 4 to 6 servings

1 **tablespoon olive oil**

1 **pound skinless, boneless chicken breasts, cut into bite-size strips**

2 **tablespoons finely chopped garlic (10 cloves)**

2 **teaspoons snipped fresh rosemary**

3 **cups chopped fresh vegetables (such as broccoli, cauliflower, zucchini, yellow summer squash, green onions, asparagus, green beans, wax beans, and/or cabbage)**

¾ **cup chicken broth**

   Hot cooked rice

½ **cup cashews**

1 Heat oil in a large skillet over medium-high heat. (If necessary, add more oil during cooking.) Add half of the chicken to the skillet. Cook and stir about 2 minutes or until chicken is no longer pink. Remove from skillet with a slotted spoon. Repeat with remaining chicken. Remove from skillet and keep warm.

2 Add garlic and rosemary to skillet. Cook and stir over medium heat about 1 minute or until fragrant. Stir in vegetables and broth. Bring to boiling; reduce heat. Cook, covered, for 3 minutes.

3 Return chicken to skillet; toss to coat. Serve chicken mixture over rice; sprinkle with cashews.

Nutrition Facts per serving: 384 cal., 13 g total fat (3 g sat. fat), 66 mg chol., 365 mg sodium, 33 g carbo., 33 g pro.

spicy stir-fried CHICKEN WITH CASHEWS

Start to Finish: 30 minutes
Makes: 4 servings

- 2 tablespoons bottled oyster sauce
- 1 tablespoon reduced-sodium soy sauce
- 1 tablespoon packed brown sugar
- 2 teaspoons cornstarch
- 1/3 cup water
- 1 tablespoon canola oil
- 2 medium red and/or green sweet peppers, seeded and cut into bite-size strips
- 1 medium onion, sliced
- 3 cups coarsely shredded bok choy or napa cabbage
- 2 to 4 fresh red hot chile peppers, seeded and finely chopped*
- 1 clove garlic, minced
- 12 ounces skinless, boneless chicken breast halves, cut into bite-size strips
- 2 cups hot cooked brown rice
- 1/4 cup lightly salted roasted cashews, coarsely chopped

1 For sauce, in a small bowl stir together oyster sauce, soy sauce, brown sugar, and cornstarch. Stir in the water. Set aside.

2 In a large wok or very large nonstick skillet heat oil over medium-high heat. Add sweet peppers and onion; stir-fry for 2 minutes. Add bok choy, chile peppers, and garlic; stir-fry for 1 to 2 minutes more or until peppers and onion are crisp-tender. Remove vegetable mixture from wok and set aside.

3 Add chicken to wok. Stir-fry for 3 to 4 minutes or until no longer pink. Push chicken to the side of wok. Stir sauce; add to wok. Cook and stir until thickened and bubbly. Return vegetable mixture to wok. Cook and stir for 1 minute more or until heated through. Serve over rice and sprinkle with cashews.

Nutrition Facts per serving: 349 cal., 10 g total fat (2 g sat. fat), 49 mg chol., 443 mg sodium, 41 g carbo., 26 g pro.

*Note: Because chile peppers contain volatile oils that can burn your skin and eyes, avoid direct contact with them as much as possible. When working with chile peppers, wear plastic or rubber gloves. If your bare hands do touch the peppers, wash your hands and nails well with soap and warm water.

kung pao CHICKEN

Prep: 25 minutes
Marinate: 15 minutes
Makes: 4 servings

12 ounces skinless, boneless
    chicken breast halves
 1 tablespoon dry sherry
 1 teaspoon cornstarch
 ¼ cup water
 ¼ cup soy sauce
 4 teaspoons cornstarch
 1 tablespoon sugar
 1 teaspoon vinegar
    Few dashes bottled hot
    pepper sauce
 1 tablespoon cooking oil
 2 teaspoons grated fresh
    ginger
 2 cloves garlic, minced
 6 green onions, cut into ½-inch
    pieces (1 cup)
 ½ cup dry roasted peanuts
 2 cups hot cooked rice
    Green onion fans (optional)

1 Cut chicken into ¾-inch pieces. In a medium bowl stir together chicken, sherry, and 1 teaspoon cornstarch. Let stand for 15 minutes.

2 For sauce, in a small bowl stir together water, soy sauce, 4 teaspoons cornstarch, sugar, vinegar, and hot pepper sauce. Set aside.

3 Pour cooking oil into a wok or large skillet. (Add more oil as necessary during cooking.) Preheat over medium-high heat. Stir-fry ginger and garlic in hot oil for 15 seconds. Add chicken mixture; stir-fry for 3 to 4 minutes or until no pink remains. Push chicken from the center of the wok.

4 Stir sauce. Add sauce to the center of the wok. Cook and stir until thickened and bubbly. Add green onion pieces and peanuts. Stir all ingredients together to coat with sauce. Cook and stir 1 to 2 minutes more or until heated through. Serve immediately with hot cooked rice. Garnish with green onion fans, if desired.

Nutrition Facts per serving: 374 cal., 15 g total fat (2 g sat. fat), 45 mg chol., 1220 mg sodium, 35 g carbo., 24 g pro.

chicken, long beans, AND TOMATO STIR-FRY

If you think good taste is hard to measure, consider Chinese long beans. A star of Asian stir-fries, these dark green, pencil-thin legumes average 1½ feet of meaty, crunchy flavor.

Start to Finish: 30 minutes
Makes: 4 servings

- 6 **ounces wide rice noodles or dried egg noodles**
- 12 **ounces skinless, boneless chicken breast halves**
- 1 **teaspoon Cajun seasoning or other spicy seasoning blend**
- 4 **teaspoons cooking oil**
- 2 **cloves garlic, minced**
- 1 **pound Chinese long beans or whole green beans, cut into 3-inch pieces**
- ¼ **cup water**
- 2 **medium tomatoes, cut into thin wedges**
- 2 **tablespoons raspberry vinegar**

❶ Cook rice noodles in boiling, lightly salted water for 3 to 5 minutes or until tender. (Or cook egg noodles according to package directions.) Drain; keep warm. Meanwhile, rinse chicken; pat dry with paper towels. Cut into thin bite-size strips. Toss chicken with Cajun seasoning. Set aside.

❷ Add 2 teaspoons of the oil to a large skillet. Preheat over medium-high heat. Stir-fry garlic in hot oil for 15 seconds. Add beans. Stir-fry for 2 minutes. Add water; reduce heat to low. Cover and simmer for 6 to 8 minutes or until beans are crisp-tender. Remove beans.

❸ Add the remaining oil to skillet. Add chicken. Stir-fry for 2 to 3 minutes or until tender and no longer pink. Return cooked beans to skillet. Add tomatoes and vinegar. Stir all ingredients together to coat. Cook and stir for 1 to 2 minutes more or until heated through. Serve immediately over noodles.

Tip: To evenly distribute garlic flavor to stir-fry ingredients, season the oil by adding the garlic first. Add the garlic to the hot oil, keeping it moving constantly so it doesn't burn. After about 15 seconds, begin adding the other stir-fry ingredients to the oil.

Nutrition Facts per serving: 361 cal., 5 g total fat (1 g sat. fat), 45 mg chol., 334 mg sodium, 54 g carbo., 25 g pro.

chicken BROCCOLI STIR-FRY

Using shredded lettuce instead of rice adds a pleasant crispness and lightness to this stir-fry.

Makes: 4 servings

12 ounces skinless, boneless chicken breast halves

 1 pound broccoli

 ½ cup chicken broth

 2 tablespoons teriyaki sauce

 2 teaspoons cornstarch

 1 teaspoon toasted sesame oil

 2 tablespoons cooking oil

 1 tablespoon grated fresh ginger

 1 clove garlic, minced

 2 cups medium fresh mushrooms, halved or quartered

 2 cups fresh bean sprouts (8 ounces)

 1 red or green sweet pepper, cut into strips

 1 8-ounce can sliced water chestnuts, drained

 4 cups coarsely shredded lettuce (optional)

1 Cut chicken into 1-inch pieces. Remove flowerets from broccoli and cut in half (you should have about 3½ cups). Cut stalks into 1½-inch lengths and then into ¼-inch strips (you should have about 1½ cups). Set aside.

2 For sauce, in a small bowl combine chicken broth, teriyaki sauce, cornstarch, and sesame oil; set aside.

3 Add cooking oil to a wok or 12-inch skillet. Preheat over medium-high heat (add more oil if necessary during cooking). Stir-fry ginger and garlic in hot oil for 15 seconds. Add the broccoli stems; stir-fry for 1 minute. Add broccoli flowerets; stir-fry for 2 to 3 minutes or until crisp-tender. Remove broccoli from wok.

4 Add mushrooms to wok; stir-fry about 1½ minutes or until crisp-tender. Remove from wok. Add bean sprouts and sweet pepper to wok; stir-fry for 1 to 2 minutes or until crisp-tender. Remove from wok. Add chicken to wok. Stir-fry for 3 to 4 minutes or until no longer pink. Push chicken from center of wok.

5 Stir sauce; add to center of wok. Cook and stir until thickened and bubbly. Return cooked vegetables to wok. Add water chestnuts. Stir all ingredients together to coat. Cook and stir about 2 minutes more or until heated through. If desired, spoon the chicken mixture over lettuce. Serve immediately.

Nutrition Facts per serving: 261 cal., 11 g total fat (2 g sat. fat), 45 mg chol., 524 mg sodium, 19 g carbo., 24 g pro.

thai CHICKEN-CURRY STIR-FRY

You can make this dish as spicy as desired by adding more or less jalapeño or serrano pepper.

Start to Finish: 30 minutes
Makes: 4 servings

⅔ **cup fat-free milk**

2 **tablespoons snipped fresh cilantro**

1 **tablespoon soy sauce**

2 **teaspoons cornstarch**

1 **teaspoon curry powder**

½ **teaspoon coconut flavoring (optional)**

¼ **teaspoon crushed red pepper**

⅛ **teaspoon salt**

12 **ounces skinless, boneless chicken breast halves**

Nonstick spray cooking

1 **large green sweet pepper, cut into 1-inch pieces**

1 **large red sweet pepper, cut into 1-inch pieces**

1 **fresh jalapeño or serrano chile pepper, seeded and finely chopped**

1 **cup sliced fresh shiitake mushrooms (stems removed)**

3 **green onions, cut into 1-inch pieces**

2 **teaspoons peanut oil or cooking oil**

3 **cups hot cooked Chinese egg noodles or rice**

Fresh cilantro (optional)

① For sauce, in a small bowl stir together the milk, snipped cilantro, soy sauce, cornstarch, curry powder, coconut flavoring (if desired), crushed red pepper, and salt. Set aside.

② Cut the chicken into bite-size strips; set aside.

③ Spray an unheated wok or large nonstick skillet with nonstick cooking. Preheat over medium heat. Add sweet peppers and jalapeño pepper; stir-fry for 2 minutes. Add mushrooms and green onions; stir-fry about 2 minutes more or until vegetables are crisp-tender. Remove from wok.

④ Add the oil to hot wok. Add chicken; stir-fry for 2 to 3 minutes or until chicken is cooked through. Push the chicken from center of wok. Stir sauce; add to center of wok. Cook and stir until thickened and bubbly.

⑤ Return vegetables to wok. Cook and stir about 1 minute more or until heated through. Serve immediately with noodles. If desired, garnish with cilantro.

Nutrition Facts per serving: 430 cal., 7 g total fat (1 g sat. fat), 83 mg chol., 394 mg sodium, 66 g carbo., 24 g pro.

sesame CHICKEN AND VEGETABLES

Prep: 30 minutes
Marinate: 1 hour
Makes: 4 servings

12 ounces skinless, boneless chicken breasts

2 tablespoons soy sauce

2 tablespoons chicken broth

2 tablespoons chopped green onion

1 tablespoon snipped parsley

1 tablespoon rice vinegar

1½ teaspoons sesame seed

1 clove garlic, minced

1½ teaspoons grated fresh ginger

1 tablespoon sesame oil

1½ cups thinly bias-sliced carrots

1 cup jicama, cut into thin, bite-size strips

6 ounces fresh medium pea pods, strings removed or one 6-ounce package frozen pea pods

Hot cooked brown rice

1 Cut chicken into bite-size strips. For marinade, in a shallow nonmetallic dish combine soy sauce, chicken broth, green onion, parsley, rice vinegar, sesame seed, garlic, and ginger. Add chicken to marinade, stirring to coat. Cover and chill for 1 hour.

2 Add 1 tablespoon sesame oil to wok or 12-inch skillet. Preheat over medium-high heat (add more oil if necessary during cooking). Stir-fry carrots in hot oil for 1 minute. Add jicama and fresh pea pods (if using); stir-fry about 2 to 3 minutes more or until crisp-tender. Remove vegetables from wok. Drain chicken, reserving marinade. Add chicken to wok; stir-fry for 2 to 3 minutes or until no longer pink. Push chicken from center of wok.

3 Add reserved marinade to center of wok. Cook and stir until bubbly. Return cooked vegetables to wok. Add frozen pea pods (if using). Stir to coat. Cook and stir about 1 minute more or until heated through. Serve immediately over hot cooked brown rice, spooning sauce over top.

Nutrition Facts per serving: 304 cal., 8 g total fat (1 g sat. fat), 45 mg chol., 621 mg sodium, 37 g carbo., 22 g pro.

peking CHICKEN STIR-FRY

Serve this ginger-flavor chicken and vegetable dish over rice or fried wonton strips. Look for the wonton wrappers next to the produce in your supermarket or any Asian grocery store.

Prep: 40 minutes
Stand: 30 minutes
Makes: 4 servings

12 dried shiitake mushrooms

12 ounces skinless, boneless chicken breasts or thighs

½ cup chicken broth

2 tablespoons soy sauce

2 tablespoons dry sherry

2 teaspoons cornstarch

¼ to ½ teaspoon chili oil or chili paste

2 tablespoons peanut oil or cooking oil

1 tablespoon grated fresh ginger

2 cloves garlic, minced

1 carrot, thinly sliced (½ cup)

3 stalks celery, cut into thin diagonal slices (1½ cups)

1 red or green sweet pepper, cut into lengthwise strips (¾ cup)

2 green onions, cut into 2-inch lengths (¼ cup)

½ of a medium bok choy, coarsely chopped (4 cups)

1½ cups pea pods, strings removed and cut into diagonal halves

1 14-ounce can baby corn, drained

Hot cooked rice

1 In a small bowl place shiitake mushrooms. Add boiling water to cover; let soak for 30 minutes. Drain; trim and discard the stems. Cut caps into halves. Set aside.

2 Meanwhile, cut chicken into bite-size strips; set aside. For sauce, stir together chicken broth, soy sauce, sherry, cornstarch, and chili oil; set aside.

3 Add peanut oil to a wok or 12-inch skillet. Preheat over medium-high heat (add more oil if necessary during cooking). Stir-fry ginger and garlic in hot oil for 15 seconds. Add carrot; stir-fry for 1 minute. Add celery; stir-fry for 1 minute. Add red sweet pepper and green onions; stir-fry for 1 to 2 minutes more or until vegetables are crisp-tender. Remove vegetables and set aside.

4 Add bok choy to wok or skillet. Stir-fry for 2 minutes. Add pea pods and reserved mushrooms; stir-fry for 1 to 2 minutes more or until crisp-tender. Remove vegetables from wok and set aside.

5 Add chicken to wok; stir-fry for 2 to 3 minutes or until no longer pink. Push chicken from center of wok. Stir sauce; add to center of wok. Cook and stir until thickened and bubbly. Return all of the cooked vegetables to wok. Add corn. Stir to coat. Cook and stir about 1 minute more or until heated through. Serve immediately over cooked rice.

Nutrition Facts per serving: 456 cal., 11 g total fat (2 g sat. fat), 45 mg chol., 386 mg sodium, 58 g carbo., 29 g pro.

asian noodles WITH CHICKEN STIR-FRY

Broccoli, cauliflower, mushrooms, and sweet pepper team up with chicken and fried bean threads for an out-of-this-world Asian meal.

Start to Finish: 35 minutes
Makes: 4 servings

3   **cups peanut oil**

2   **ounces bean thread vermicelli**

12   **ounces skinless, boneless chicken breasts or thighs**

¾   **cup chicken broth**

2   **tablespoons teriyaki sauce**

4   **teaspoons cornstarch**

1   **tablespoon cooking oil**

2   **tablespoons finely chopped lemongrass or 1 teaspoon finely shredded lemon peel**

2   **cloves garlic, minced**

2   **cups broccoli flowerets**

1   **cup cauliflower flowerets**

4   **ounces fresh shiitake mushrooms, stems removed and sliced**

1   **red or green sweet pepper, cut into 1-inch squares**

8   **green onions, cut into 2-inch lengths**

2   **medium tomatoes, cut into wedges**

    Snipped cilantro or parsley (optional)

1 In a wok or 12-inch skillet heat the 3 cups peanut oil to 375°F. Add the vermicelli to hot oil and cook about 8 seconds or until puffed, turning once. (Do not let brown.) Drain on paper towels; set aside. Cool and discard peanut oil.

2 Cut chicken into 1-inch pieces; set aside.

3 For sauce, in a small bowl combine chicken broth, teriyaki sauce, and cornstarch; set aside.

4 Add 1 tablespoon cooking oil to the same wok or a 12-inch skillet. Preheat over medium-high heat (add more oil if necessary during cooking). Stir-fry lemongrass and garlic in hot oil for 15 seconds. Add broccoli and cauliflower; stir-fry for 2 minutes. Add mushrooms, red sweet pepper, and green onions; stir-fry for 1½ to 2 minutes more or until vegetables are crisp-tender. Remove vegetables from wok. Add chicken to wok; stir-fry about 4 minutes or until no longer pink. Push chicken from center of wok.

5 Stir sauce; add to center of wok. Cook and stir until thickened and bubbly. Return cooked vegetables to wok. Add tomatoes. Stir to coat. Cook and stir about 2 minutes more or until heated through. Serve immediately with vermicelli. Sprinkle with cilantro or parsley, if desired.

Nutrition Facts per serving: 386 cal., 20 g total fat (4 g sat. fat), 45 mg chol., 658 mg sodium, 30 g carbo., 24 g pro.

chicken WITH FRESH PINEAPPLE

Add to the tropical feel of this Asian-style chicken dish by garnishing with wedges of fresh pineapple.

Start to Finish: 25 minutes
Makes: 4 servings

- 12 ounces skinless, boneless chicken thighs or breasts
- ⅓ cup unsweetened pineapple juice
- ¼ cup orange juice
- 1½ teaspoons cornstarch
- ¼ teaspoon crushed red pepper
- 1 tablespoon cooking oil
- 2 cloves garlic, minced
- 1 medium green sweet pepper, cut into 1-inch squares (1 cup)
- 4 green onions, cut into 2-inch pieces
- ½ medium pineapple, peeled, cored, and cut into 1-inch chunks (1½ cups)
  Hot cooked rice
- ¼ cup coarsely chopped cashews

1 Cut chicken into thin, bite-size strips. Set aside.

2 For sauce, in a small bowl combine pineapple juice, orange juice, cornstarch, and crushed red pepper. Set aside.

3 Add oil to wok or 12-inch skillet. Preheat over medium-high heat (add more oil if necessary during cooking). Stir-fry garlic in hot oil for 15 seconds. Add green sweet pepper and green onions. Stir-fry for 1½ minutes. Remove vegetables from the wok.

4 Add chicken to wok. Stir-fry chicken for 2 to 3 minutes or until no longer pink. Push chicken from center of wok. Stir sauce; add to center of wok. Cook and stir until thickened and bubbly. Return cooked vegetables to wok. Add pineapple. Stir to coat. Cook and stir about 1 minute more or until heated through. Serve immediately over cooked rice. Sprinkle with cashews.

Nutrition Facts per serving: 359 cal., 10 g total fat (2 g sat. fat), 45 mg chol., 96 mg sodium, 45 g carbo., 21 g pro.

grilled
AND BROILED

Chili-Rubbed Chicken Thighs, *page 181*

chicken WITH CHIPOTLE BARBECUE SAUCE

Chipotle chile peppers are dried, smoked jalapeño peppers with a smoky, sweet, almost chocolaty flavor. They're available simply dried or canned in a spicy, chili-flavored adobo paste. Any remaining canned chipotle peppers may be frozen in an airtight container for up to three months.

Prep: 30 minutes
Grill: 12 minutes
Makes: 6 servings

¼ **cup canned chipotle peppers in adobo sauce**

Nonstick cooking spray

⅓ **cup finely chopped onion**

3 **cloves garlic, minced**

1 **cup ketchup**

3 **tablespoons white wine vinegar**

3 **tablespoons molasses or sorghum**

1 **tablespoon Worcestershire sauce**

6 **medium skinless, boneless chicken breast halves (about 1½ pounds total)**

1 For sauce, remove any stems from chipotle peppers. Place peppers and adobo sauce in a blender container. Cover and blend until smooth. Set aside.

2 Coat a medium saucepan with cooking spray. Heat saucepan over medium heat. Add onion and garlic; cook until onion is tender. Stir in pureed chipotle peppers, ketchup, vinegar, molasses, and Worcestershire sauce. Bring to boiling; reduce heat. Simmer, uncovered, about 10 minutes or until sauce is slightly thickened.

3 Grill chicken on the rack of an uncovered grill directly over medium coals for 12 to 15 minutes or until chicken is tender and no longer pink, turning once and brushing occasionally with some of the sauce the last 5 minutes of grilling.

4 To serve, bring the remaining sauce to boiling. Serve the sauce with chicken.

Nutrition Facts per serving: 291 cal., 6 g total fat (1 g sat. fat), 59 mg chol., 1,399 mg sodium, 36 g carbo., 23 g pro.

basil-and-garlic-stuffed
CHICKEN BREASTS

Prep: 20 minutes
Grill: 25 minutes
Makes: 4 servings

¼ **cup grated Parmesan cheese**

2 **tablespoons snipped fresh basil**

1 **tablespoon olive oil**

2 **cloves garlic, minced**

4 **skinless, boneless chicken breast halves**

½ **teaspoon finely shredded lemon peel**

2 **tablespoons lemon juice**

1 **tablespoon olive oil**

1 In a small bowl combine Parmesan cheese, basil, 1 tablespoon olive oil, and garlic; set aside.

2 Place each chicken breast half between two pieces of plastic wrap. Using the flat side of a meat mallet, pound lightly to about ⅛-inch thickness. Remove plastic wrap. Spread cheese mixture on chicken. Fold in sides of each chicken breast; roll up, pressing edges to seal. Fasten with wooden toothpicks.

3 For sauce, in a small bowl combine lemon peel, lemon juice, and 1 tablespoon olive oil; set aside.

4 For a charcoal grill, arrange medium-hot coals around a drip pan. Test for medium heat above pan. Place chicken on the grill rack over drip pan. Cover and grill for 25 to 30 minutes or until chicken is no longer pink (170°F), brushing occasionally with sauce the last 10 minutes of grilling. (For a gas grill, preheat grill. Reduce heat to medium. Adjust grill for indirect cooking. Grill as above.)

Nutrition Facts per serving: 273 cal., 10 g total fat (2 g sat. fat), 103 mg chol., 188 mg sodium, 1 g carbo., 41 g pro.

grilled CHICKEN AND CREAMY CORN

Start to Finish: 20 minutes
Makes: 4 servings

- 2 tablespoons olive oil
- 1 teaspoon smoked paprika
- 3 fresh ears of sweet corn
- 4 skinless, boneless chicken breast halves
- ⅓ cup sour cream
  Milk
- ¼ cup shredded fresh basil

① In small bowl combine olive oil and paprika. Brush corn and chicken with oil mixture. Lightly sprinkle salt and pepper. Grill directly over medium coals for 12 to 15 minutes or until chicken is no longer pink (170°F), turning once.

② Carefully cut kernels from cob by firmly holding the corn at the top (using a kitchen towel to grip, if necessary) and slicing downward with a sharp knife. Transfer to bowl; stir in sour cream. Season with additional salt and pepper. Stir in milk to desired creaminess. Slice chicken breasts. Serve with corn; sprinkle shredded basil.

Nutrition Facts per serving: 309 cal., 13 g total fat (4 g sat. fat), 89 mg chol., 238 mg sodium, 14 g carbo., 36 g pro.

grilled CHICKEN SALAD

This Greek-inspired dish features lemon- and oregano-marinated grilled chicken tossed with a crunchy mix of cucumbers, tomatoes, and onion. In keeping with the Greek theme, there's also creamy cucumber salad dressing, feta cheese, and kalamata olives.

Prep: 30 minutes
Marinate: 4 to 24 hours
Grill: 12 minutes
Makes: 4 servings

4 **skinless, boneless chicken breast halves (1¼ to 1½ pounds total)**

1 **tablespoon lemon juice**

1 **tablespoon olive oil**

1 **tablespoon snipped fresh oregano or 1 teaspoon dried oregano, crushed**

¼ **teaspoon black pepper**

2 **cloves garlic, minced**

3 **medium cucumbers, seeded and cut into ½-inch pieces**

2 **medium tomatoes, cut into ½-inch pieces**

½ **cup chopped red onion (1 medium)**

Mixed salad greens (optional)

⅓ **cup bottled reduced-calorie creamy cucumber salad dressing**

½ **cup crumbled feta cheese**

¼ **cup chopped pitted kalamata olives or ripe olives**

1 Place chicken in a resealable plastic bag set in a shallow dish. For marinade, in a small bowl combine lemon juice, oil, oregano, pepper, and garlic. Pour over chicken; seal bag. Marinate in the refrigerator for at least 4 hours or up to 24 hours, turning bag occasionally.

2 Meanwhile, in a medium bowl toss together cucumbers, tomatoes, and red onion.

3 Drain chicken, discarding marinade. Place chicken on the rack of an uncovered grill directly over medium coals. Grill for 12 to 15 minutes or until tender and no longer pink (170°F), turning once.

4 Transfer chicken to a cutting board; cut into bite-size pieces. Toss with cucumber mixture. If desired, serve on greens. Drizzle salad dressing over. Sprinkle with feta cheese and olives.

Nutrition Facts per serving: 328 cal., 13 g total fat (3 g sat. fat), 95 mg chol., 629 mg sodium, 14 g carbo., 37 g pro.

chicken AND ROASTED PEPPER SANDWICHES

Prep: 15 minutes
Marinate: 15 minutes
Grill: 4 minutes (covered) or
      10 minutes (uncovered)
Makes: 4 sandwiches

¼ **cup olive oil**

4 **teaspoons red wine vinegar**

1 **tablespoon snipped fresh
   thyme**

½ **teaspoon salt**

¼ **teaspoon crushed red pepper**

4 **skinless, boneless chicken
   breast halves**

4 **1-inch bias-cut slices Italian
   bread**

¼ **cup semisoft cheese with
   herbs or semisoft goat
   cheese (chèvre)**

1 **cup roasted red sweet
   peppers (about one 7-ounce
   jar), cut into strips**

½ **cup fresh basil, watercress, or
   baby spinach leaves**

1 For marinade, in a small bowl whisk together oil, vinegar, thyme, salt, and crushed red pepper. Reserve 2 tablespoons of mixture; set aside.

2 Place chicken between two sheets of plastic wrap; pound lightly with the flat side of a meat mallet to about ½-inch thickness. Place in a resealable plastic bag set in a shallow dish. Add remaining marinade; seal bag. Marinate at room temperature about 15 minutes or in the refrigerator for up to 1 hour.

3 Lightly grease the rack of an indoor electric grill or lightly coat with nonstick cooking spray. Preheat grill. Drain chicken, discarding marinade. Place chicken on the grill rack. If using a covered grill, close the lid. Grill until chicken is no longer pink (170°F). For a covered grill, allow 3 to 4 minutes. For an uncovered grill, allow 8 to 10 minutes, turning once halfway through grilling.

4 Brush cut sides of bread with reserved marinade. Place bread, cut sides down, on grill rack. If using a covered grill, close the lid. Grill until lightly toasted. For a covered grill, allow 1 to 2 minutes. For an uncovered grill, allow 2 to 4 minutes, turning once halfway through grilling. Remove bread from grill.

5 To serve, place a chicken breast on each grilled bread slice. Spread with cheese. Top each sandwich with sweet peppers and basil.

Nutrition Facts per sandwich: 418 cal., 20 g total fat (5 g sat. fat), 82 mg chol., 629 mg sodium, 21 g carbo., 37 g pro.

grilled chicken CAESAR

Watercress is a tender green with a peppery bite. Substitute baby arugula, if desired.

Prep: 20 minutes
Grill: 8 minutes
Makes: 4 servings

- 1 tablespoon fresh lemon juice
- 1 teaspoon anchovy paste
- ¼ teaspoon freshly ground black pepper
- 2 tablespoons olive oil
- 1 tablespoon finely chopped shallot
- 4 skinless, boneless chicken breast halves (1¼ pounds)
- 4 cups trimmed watercress
  Lemon wedges (optional)

1 For dressing, in a small bowl whisk together lemon juice, anchovy paste, and the ¼ teaspoon pepper; whisk in olive oil and shallot. Set aside.

2 Place each chicken breast half between two pieces of plastic wrap. Pound lightly with the flat side of a meat mallet to ¼-inch thickness. Discard plastic wrap. Lightly sprinkle chicken with salt and pepper.

3 Place chicken on the rack of an uncovered grill directly over medium heat. Grill for 8 to 10 minutes or until chicken is no longer pink, turning once halfway through grilling.

4 Meanwhile, toss watercress with dressing; arrange on four plates. Top with chicken. If desired, garnish with lemon wedges.

Nutrition Facts per serving: 240 cal., 11 g total fat (2 g sat. fat), 89 mg chol., 146 mg sodium, 1 g carbo., 33 g pro.

grilled vietnamese CHICKEN BREASTS

This is no ho-hum chicken sandwich. Spicy-sweet peanut sauce and crisp broccoli slaw lend an Asian accent to this out-of-the ordinary grilled chicken.

Prep: 15 minutes
Grill: 12 minutes
Makes: 4 servings

- 4 **medium skinless, boneless chicken breast halves (about 1 pound total)**
- 2 **teaspoons toasted sesame oil**
- ½ **teaspoon crushed red pepper**
- 2 **tablespoons sugar**
- 2 **tablespoons peanut butter**
- 2 **tablespoons soy sauce**
- 1 **tablespoon cooking oil**
- 1 **clove garlic, minced**
- 4 **French-style rolls, split**
- ¼ **cup radish sprouts**
- ½ **cup packaged shredded broccoli (broccoli slaw mix)**
- ¼ **cup chopped peanuts (optional)**

1 Rinse chicken; pat dry. Combine sesame oil and crushed red pepper; brush over chicken.

2 Grill chicken on the lightly greased rack of an uncovered grill directly over medium heat for 12 to 15 minutes or until tender and no longer pink, turning once.

3 Meanwhile, for sauce, in a small saucepan* stir together sugar, peanut butter, soy sauce, oil, garlic, and 2 tablespoons water. Heat on grill rack until sugar is dissolved, stirring frequently. For the last 1 minute of grilling, place split rolls on the grill rack to toast.

4 To serve, place cooked chicken breasts on bottom halves of rolls; spoon on sauce and top with radish sprouts, broccoli, peanuts (if desired), and roll tops.

Nutrition Facts per serving: 360 cal., 14 g total fat (3 g sat. fat), 59 mg chol., 852 mg sodium, 29 g carbo., 28 g pro.

*Note: The heat from the grill will blacken the outside of the saucepan, so use an old one or a small cast-iron skillet.

chicken and kiwi TACOS

A colorful kiwifruit-and-tomato relish adds a fresh note to these cumin-seasoned chicken tacos.

Prep: 25 minutes
Grill: 6 minutes
Makes: 6 tacos

½ teaspoon ground cumin

¼ teaspoon salt

⅛ to ¼ teaspoon crushed red pepper

8 ounces skinless, boneless chicken breast halves

1 teaspoon cooking oil

6 taco shells

1 cup shredded romaine lettuce

½ cup shredded Monterey Jack cheese or pepper Jack cheese (2 ounces)

3 kiwifruit, peeled and chopped

1 small tomato, chopped

1 tablespoon lime or lemon juice

1 Combine cumin, salt, and red pepper in a small bowl. Brush chicken breasts with oil. Rub brushed chicken breasts with cumin mixture. Place each breast half between two pieces of plastic wrap; gently pound with a meat mallet to ½ inch thickness.

2 Place chicken on the lightly oiled rack of an uncovered grill directly over medium-high heat. Grill for 6 to 8 minutes or until an instant-read thermometer registers 170°F and juices run clear, turning once. Remove chicken; set aside until cool enough to handle. Meanwhile, if using purchased taco shells, heat shells according to the package directions.

3 Cut chicken into thin strips and arrange in taco shells.* Top with lettuce and cheese. Toss together chopped kiwifruit, tomato, and lime juice in a small bowl. Sprinkle atop tacos.

Nutrition Facts per serving: 170 cal., 7 g total fat (3 g sat. fat), 30 mg chol., 219 mg sodium, 13 g carbo., 13 g pro.

*Test Kitchen Tip: To make taco shells, heat ½ inch of cooking oil in a large, heavy skillet. Cook six 5-inch tortillas, one at a time, in hot oil until just golden. Remove from hot oil with tongs. Fold over a paper-towel-lined rolling pin or wire tortilla rack placed over a paper-towel-lined plate. Let cool until firm.

barbecued CHICKEN THIGHS

Thread chunks of red sweet pepper, corn on the cob, and zucchini on skewers for a quick partner to grill with the chicken thighs.

Prep: 15 minutes
Grill: 15 minutes
Makes: 4 servings

- 3 tablespoons brown sugar
- 2 tablespoons finely chopped onion
- 2 tablespoons vinegar
- 2 tablespoons prepared mustard
- ¼ teaspoon celery seeds
- ⅛ teaspoon garlic powder
- 8 chicken thighs (about 2½ pounds total)
- ½ teaspoon paprika
- ¼ teaspoon ground turmeric
- ¼ teaspoon salt

1 For sauce, in a small saucepan combine brown sugar, onion, vinegar, mustard, celery seed, and garlic powder. Bring to boiling, stirring until the sugar dissolves. Remove from heat; set aside.

2 Skin chicken, if desired. In a small mixing bowl combine paprika, turmeric, and salt; rub over the chicken.

3 Grill chicken on an uncovered grill directly over medium coals for 20 minutes. Turn chicken; grill for 15 to 20 minutes more or until chicken is tender and no longer pink. (Or place chicken on the unheated rack of a broiler pan. Broil 5 to 6 inches from the heat for 28 to 32 minutes, turning once.) Brush with sauce during the last 5 minutes of grilling or broiling.

Nutrition Facts per serving: 375 cal., 19 g total fat (5 g sat. fat), 129 mg chol., 366 mg sodium, 11 g carbo., 37 g pro.

Make Ahead: Prepare sauce up to 48 hours ahead; cover and chill.

chili-rubbed CHICKEN THIGHS

Chicken thighs take well to an assertive rub of hot chili powder. Serve them with the easiest-ever potatoes.

Prep: 15 minutes
Microwave: 10 minutes
Grill: potatoes for 45 to 60 minutes; chicken thighs for 6 minutes
Makes: 4 servings

Spice Rub*

4 **baking potatoes (about 6 ounces each), scrubbed and blotted dry**

1 **medium-size onion, thinly sliced**

4 **tablespoons butter**

8 **bone-in chicken thighs (about 2½ pounds total)**

① Prepare Spice Rub. Set aside.

② Heat gas grill to medium-high or prepare charcoal grill with medium-hot coals. Cut each potato in half lengthwise. With a paring knife, score flesh of the potato crosswise in a criss-cross fashion. Place one-quarter of the onion, 1 tablespoon butter and ½ teaspoon of the spice rub between the halves of each potato. Press halves together; seal tightly in a double layer of aluminum foil. Place foil packets on grill over indirect heat; close lid. Grill for 45 to 60 minutes or until tender.

③ Remove skin from chicken thighs. Coat both sides of chicken with remaining spice rub. Place chicken in a 13x9-inch microwave-safe baking dish. Cover with plastic wrap and vent in one corner. Microwave on high for 10 minutes.

④ Grill thighs about 3 minutes per side or until instant-read meat thermometer inserted in thigh (not touching bone) registers 170°F. Serve chicken thighs with grilled potatoes.

***Spice Rub:** In small bowl, stir together ¼ cup paprika, 1 tablespoon dark brown sugar, 2 teaspoons hot chili powder, 1 teaspoon ground cumin, 1 teaspoon garlic salt, and 1 teaspoon salt.

Nutrition Facts per serving: 624 cal., 28 g total fat (12 g sat. fat), 162 mg chol., 886 mg sodium, 53 g carbo., 41 g pro.

dipping DRUMSTICKS

Kids love to dip! Try these easy-fixing drumsticks or chicken breast halves, and let your kids choose their favorite dipping sauces.

Prep: 15 minutes
Grill: 50 minutes
Makes: 4 servings

3 **tablespoons white wine Worcestershire sauce**

2 **cloves garlic, minced**

½ **teaspoon poultry seasoning**

⅛ **teaspoon ground black pepper**

8 **chicken drumsticks***

Assorted dipping sauces (such as bottled ranch salad dressing, barbecue sauce, sweet-and-sour sauce, or creamy Dijon-style mustard blend)

1 In a small bowl combine Worcestershire sauce, garlic, poultry seasoning, and pepper. Remove the skin from chicken. Brush chicken with Worcestershire mixture.

2 For a charcoal grill, arrange medium-hot coals around a drip pan. Test for medium heat above the pan. Place chicken on the grill rack over the drip pan. Grill, covered, for 50 to 60 minutes or until chicken is no longer pink (180°F), turning once halfway through grilling. (For a gas grill. Preheat grill. Reduce heat to medium. Adjust heat for indirect cooking. Grill as above.)

3 Serve drumsticks with desired dipping sauces.

Nutrition Facts per serving: 371 cal., 27 g total fat (6 g sat. fat), 127 mg chol., 562 mg sodium, 5 g carbo., 28 g pro.

*Note: If you prefer, use 4 skinless, boneless chicken breast halves (about 1¼ pounds total). Prepare as directed in Step 1. Place chicken breast halves on the grill rack directly over medium heat; grill for 12 to 15 minutes or until tender and no longer pink (170°F), turning once halfway through grilling. Cut chicken breasts into 1-inch-wide strips. Serve with desired dipping sauces.

southwest-style CHICKEN BURGERS

These burgers are like a taco in a bun. For a boost in seasoning, use nacho-flavor tortilla chips.

Prep: 20 minutes
Broil: 15 minutes
Makes: 4 servings

- 1 **slightly beaten egg**
- ¼ **cup finely crushed nacho-flavor or plain tortilla chips**
- 3 **tablespoons finely chopped green sweet pepper**
- ¾ **teaspoon chili powder**
- ¼ **teaspoon salt**
- ¼ **teaspoon black pepper**
- 1 **pound uncooked ground chicken**
- 2 **ounces Monterey Jack cheese with jalapeño peppers, sliced**
- 4 **kaiser rolls or hamburger buns, split and toasted**
- 1 **avocado, halved, seeded, peeled, and sliced**
- 4 **lettuce leaves**
- ¼ **cup bottled salsa**

1 In a medium bowl combine egg, tortilla chips, sweet pepper, chili powder, salt, and black pepper. Add chicken; mix well. (Mixture will be wet.) Shape chicken mixture into four ¾-inch-thick round patties.

2 Place patties on the unheated rack of a broiler pan. Broil 4 inches from the heat for 14 to 18 minutes or until no longer pink and an instant-read thermometer registers 165°F, turning once halfway through broiling time. Top burgers with cheese. Broil for 1 minute more or until cheese melts.

3 Serve burgers on toasted rolls; top with avocado slices, lettuce, and salsa.

Nutrition Facts per serving: 522 cal., 26 g total fat (5 g sat. fat), 66 mg chol., 698 mg sodium, 39 g carbo., 32 g pro.

chicken burgers WITH
RANCH COLESLAW

Your family will love this tender and succulent chicken burger topped with ranch coleslaw mix.

Prep: 35 minutes
Grill: 10 minutes
Makes: 4 servings

- 3   cups packaged coleslaw mix
- ½   cup prepared ranch salad dressing
- ¼   teaspoon grated lemon peel
- 1   tablespoon butter or margarine
- ½   cup minced onion
- 1¼ pounds ground chicken
- ½   cup shredded zucchini
- ½   cup shredded Swiss cheese
- ½   teaspoon salt
- ¼   teaspoon freshly ground black pepper
- 4   kaiser rolls, split

1. Heat grill.

2. In a medium bowl combine the coleslaw mix, dressing, and lemon peel; cover and refrigerate 30 minutes.

3. Melt butter in medium skillet over medium-high heat. Add onion and cook 4 to 5 minutes or until browned. Remove from heat; cool.

4. Cover a cookie sheet with plastic wrap. Lightly mix chicken, cooked onion, zucchini, cheese, salt, and pepper in large bowl just until combined. Drop 4 equal mounds of chicken mixture on prepared sheet. Cover with another piece of plastic wrap and gently press mounds into four ½-inch-thick patties.

5. Grill burgers over medium-hot heat about 5 minutes per side or until browned and an instant-read meat thermometer inserted in side of burger registers 165°F.*

6. Meanwhile, grill rolls cut sides down until toasted, about 1 minute. Arrange burgers on bottoms of rolls. Divide coleslaw among burgers; top with roll tops.

Nutrition Facts per serving: 645 cal., 38.5 g total fat (10.5 g sat. fat), 146 mg chol., 1,088 mg sodium, 38 g carbo., 36 g pro.

*Note: The internal color of burgers is not a reliable doneness indicator. Ground chicken burgers must be cooked to 165°F. An instant-read meat thermometer ensures perfectly cooked burgers. If using digital instant-read thermometer, insert the tip of the thermometer into the food at least ¼ of an inch for 10 seconds. If using a dial instant-read thermometer, insert the thermometer through the side of the burger to a depth of 2 to 3 inches to get an accurate reading.

chicken burgers WITH
PINEAPPLE SALSA

This fruity salsa dresses up grilled chicken patties.

Prep: 25 minutes
Grill: 14 minutes
Makes: 4 servings

- 1 **8.25-ounce can crushed pineapple, drained**
- ½ **cup chopped red or green sweet pepper**
- ½ **cup sliced green onion**
- 2 **tablespoons snipped fresh cilantro or parsley**
- 2 **cloves garlic, minced**
- 1 **jalapeño or serrano pepper, seeded and finely chopped***
- 1 **egg**
- ¼ **cup fine dry bread crumbs**
- 1 **teaspoon dried basil, crushed**
- ½ **teaspoon ground sage**
- ½ **teaspoon seasoned salt**
- ⅛ **teaspoon pepper**
- 1 **pound uncooked ground chicken or turkey**

1 Preheat grill. For salsa, in a medium bowl combine crushed pineapple, sweet pepper, half of the green onion, the cilantro, garlic, and jalapeño pepper. Cover; chill until serving time.

2 In another medium bowl combine the egg, bread crumbs, remaining onion, basil, sage, seasoned salt, and pepper. Add ground chicken; mix well. Shape into four ¾-inch-thick patties. Grill patties on the grill rack of an uncovered grill directly over medium coals for 14 to 18 minutes or until juices run clear and an instant-read thermometer inserted in side of burger registers 165° F, turning halfway through grilling. (Or preheat broiler. Broil 4 to 5 inches from heat on an unheated rack of broiler pan for 10 to 12 minutes.) Serve burgers with salsa.

Nutrition Facts per serving: 228 cal., 10 g total fat (3 g sat. fat), 95 mg chol., 273 mg sodium, 16 g carbo., 18 g pro.

***Note:** Because hot peppers contain oils that can burn your eyes, lips, and skin, protect yourself when working with peppers by wearing plastic gloves or bags. Be sure to wash your hands thoroughly before touching your eyes or face.

Make Ahead: Prepare salsa; cover and chill up to 8 hours.

basil-chicken BURGERS

Prep: 15 minutes
Grill: 10 minutes
Makes: 4 servings

¼ cup snipped fresh basil

¼ cup fine dry bread crumbs

4 teaspoons Worcestershire
    sauce

⅛ teaspoon salt

⅛ teaspoon black pepper

1 pound uncooked ground
    chicken

8 slices French bread,
    toasted, or 4 kaiser rolls or
    hamburger buns, split and
    toasted

   Assorted condiments (such
    as lettuce leaves, sliced
    tomato, and/or sliced onion)
    (optional)

1 In a large bowl combine basil, bread crumbs, Worcestershire sauce, salt, and pepper. Add ground chicken; mix well. Shape chicken mixture into four ½-inch-thick patties. (The mixture may be sticky. If necessary, wet hands to shape patties.)

2 For a charcoal grill, grill burgers on the rack of an uncovered grill directly over medium coals for 10 to 13 minutes or until no longer pink (170°F), turning once halfway through grilling. (For a gas grill, preheat grill. Reduce heat to medium. Place burgers on grill rack over heat. Cover and grill as above.)

3 Serve burgers on French bread. If desired, serve with assorted condiments.

Nutrition Facts per serving: 334 cal., 11 g total fat (0 g sat. fat), 0 mg chol., 678 mg sodium, 32 g carbo., 25 g pro.

apple-glazed CHICKEN WITH SPINACH

Prep: 20 minutes
Broil: 12 minutes
Makes: 4 servings

½ cup apple jelly

2 tablespoons soy sauce

1 tablespoon snipped fresh thyme

1 teaspoon finely shredded lemon peel

1 teaspoon grated fresh ginger

4 skinless, boneless chicken breast halves (about 1 pound total)

Nonstick cooking spray

2 medium apples, peeled, cored, and chopped

⅓ cup sliced leek

2 cloves garlic, minced

2 tablespoons apple cider or chicken broth

1 10-ounce package prewashed spinach, trimmed (about 8 cups)

Salt and ground black pepper

① For glaze, in a small saucepan heat apple jelly, soy sauce, thyme, lemon peel, and ginger just until jelly is melted. Set aside ¼ cup of the glaze.

② Preheat broiler. Place chicken on the unheated rack of a broiler pan. Broil 4 to 5 inches from the heat for 12 to 15 minutes or until chicken is no longer pink (170°F), turning once and brushing with the remaining glaze the last 5 minutes of broiling. (Or place chicken on the rack of an uncovered grill directly over medium coals. Grill for 12 to 15 minutes, turning once and brushing with the remaining glaze the last 5 minutes of grilling.)

③ Meanwhile, lightly coat a large saucepan or Dutch oven with cooking spray. Heat saucepan over medium heat. Add apples, leek, and garlic; cook for 3 minutes. Add the reserved ¼ cup glaze and apple cider; bring to boiling. Add spinach; toss just until wilted. Season to taste with salt and black pepper.

④ To serve, cut each chicken piece crosswise into 6 to 8 slices. Divide the spinach mixture among dinner plates. Top with sliced chicken.

Nutrition Facts per serving: 263 cal., 3 g total fat (1 g sat. fat), 45 mg chol., 654 mg sodium, 42 g carbo., 19 g pro.

lemon-dill BUTTER CHICKEN AND CUCUMBERS

Cook the cucumber until it just begins to soften, but still retains a bit of crispness. If you like, seed the cucumber before chopping it.

Prep: 10 minutes
Broil: 12 minutes
Makes: 4 servings

- 4 **skinless, boneless chicken breast halves**
- 1 **medium lemon**
- 3 **tablespoons butter**
- ½ **teaspoon dried dill**
- ¼ **teaspoon salt**
- ¼ **teaspoon ground black pepper**
- 1½ **cups coarsely chopped cucumber or zucchini**

1 Preheat broiler. Place chicken on the unheated rack of a broiler pan. Broil 4 to 5 inches from heat for 12 to 15 minutes or until no longer pink (170°F), turning once halfway through broiling.

2 Meanwhile, finely shred ½ teaspoon peel from the lemon. Cut lemon in half; squeeze lemon to get 2 tablespoons juice.

3 In a small skillet melt butter over medium heat. Stir in lemon peel, lemon juice, dill, salt, and pepper. Stir in cucumber. Cook and stir over medium heat for 3 to 4 minutes or until cucumber is just tender. Spoon sauce over chicken.

Nutrition Facts per serving: 244 cal., 11 g total fat (6 g sat. fat), 107 mg chol., 477 mg sodium, 2 g carbo., 33 g pro.

broiled CHILI-GLAZED CHICKEN AND PEPPERS

Makes: 4 servings

- **4 skinless, boneless chicken breast halves (about 1 pound total)**
- **2 medium red, yellow, or green sweet peppers**
- **¼ cup chili sauce**
- **2 tablespoons bottled barbecue sauce**
- **1 tablespoon snipped fresh cilantro or parsley**

1 Preheat broiler. Rinse chicken; pat dry. Place chicken pieces on the unheated rack of a broiler pan. Halve peppers from stem to tip; remove center core. Cut each half into 4 wedges. Place peppers, cut side down, on broiler pan. In a small bowl stir together chili sauce, barbecue sauce, and cilantro.

2 Brush chicken and pepper pieces lightly with chili sauce mixture. Broil 4 to 5 inches from heat for 5 minutes; turn and brush generously with sauce mixture. Broil for 4 to 6 minutes more or until chicken is tender and no longer pink, brushing once or twice more with sauce during cooking. Serve each piece of chicken with 4 pepper wedges. If desired, garnish with sprigs of cilantro.

Nutrition Facts per serving: 153 cal., 3 g total fat (1 g sat. fat), 59 mg chol., 319 mg sodium, 7 g carbo., 23 g pro.

middle eastern CHICKEN KABOBS

Prep: 25 minutes
Marinate: 1 hour
Broil: 8 minutes
Makes: 6 servings

1 **pound skinless, boneless chicken breast halves, cut into 1-inch pieces**

¼ **cup plain low-fat yogurt**

1 **tablespoon lemon juice**

1 **teaspoon dry mustard**

1 **teaspoon ground cinnamon**

1 **teaspoon curry powder**

½ **teaspoon salt**

¼ **to ½ teaspoon crushed red pepper**

1 **large red sweet pepper, cut into 1-inch pieces (1 cup)**

1 **medium yellow summer squash, halved lengthwise and cut into ½-inch-thick slices**

Soft pita breads, warmed (optional)

Tomato Relish* (optional)

1 Place chicken in a resealable plastic bag set in a bowl. In a small bowl stir together yogurt, lemon juice, mustard, cinnamon, curry powder, salt, and crushed red pepper. Pour over chicken. Seal bag; turn to coat. Refrigerate for 1 to 4 hours, turning occasionally.

2 Preheat broiler. On six long metal skewers, thread chicken, sweet pepper, and squash, leaving ¼ inch between pieces. Broil 4 to 5 inches from heat for 8 to 10 minutes or until chicken is no longer pink, turning once. If desired, serve with pita bread and Tomato Relish.

***Tomato Relish:** Combine 2 roma tomatoes, chopped; ½ cup grape tomatoes, halved; 1 tablespoon balsamic vinegar; 1 teaspoon snipped fresh oregano; 1 teaspoon snipped fresh thyme; 1 teaspoon honey; and 1 clove garlic, minced. Add salt and ground black pepper to taste. Cover; chill up to 4 hours.

Nutrition Facts per serving: 107 cal., 2 g total fat (0 g sat. fat), 44 mg chol., 254 mg sodium, 4 g carbo., 19 g pro.

broiled CHICKEN WITH GARLIC-SAUCE

Makes: 4 servings

4 skinless, boneless chicken breast halves (about 1 pound total)

2 tablespoons olive oil or cooking oil

½ cup mayonnaise or salad dressing

2 tablespoons milk

1 tablespoon snipped fresh chives or 1 teaspoon dried chives

1½ teaspoon bottled minced garlic

1 teaspoon lemon juice

¼ teaspoon pepper

¼ teaspoon dry mustard

Lemon wedges (optional)

Fresh chives (optional)

1 Preheat broiler. Rinse chicken; pat dry. Place chicken pieces in the unheated rack of a broiler pan. Brush with 1 tablespoon of the olive oil. Broil 4 to 5 inches from the heat for 5 minutes.

2 Meanwhile, stir together mayonnaise, milk, chives, garlic, lemon juice, pepper, and mustard.

3 Turn chicken; brush with remaining oil. Broil 4 to 6 minutes more or until chicken is tender and no longer pink. Transfer chicken to heated platter. Spoon some of the garlic sauce over chicken; serve immediately. Pass remaining sauce. Garnish with lemon wedges and fresh chives, if desired.

Nutrition Facts per serving: 387 cal., 32 g total fat (5 g sat. fat), 76 mg chol., 215 mg sodium, 2 g carbo., 22 g pro.

broiled chicken thighs
WITH HONEY-APRICOT GLAZE

To vary the flavor of the sweet-sour glaze, substitute other preserves for the apricot, such as plum or raspberry, or try orange marmalade.

Broil: 8 to 11 minutes
Makes: 4 servings

- 1 **pound skinless, boneless chicken breast halves**
- 1 **tablespoon olive oil or cooking oil**
- ¼ **teaspoon garlic salt**
- ⅛ **teaspoon pepper**
- ¼ **cup apricot preserves**
- 1 **tablespoon honey**
- 2 **tablespoons vinegar**
  Cooked carrots (optional)

1 Preheat broiler. Rinse chicken; pat dry. Place chicken pieces on unheated rack of a broiler pan. Brush with oil and sprinkle with garlic salt and pepper. Broil 4 to 5 inches from the heat for 5 minutes.

2 Meanwhile in a small saucepan stir apricot preserves and honey over medium heat until mixture is melted. Remove from heat; stir in vinegar. Brush mixture over chicken pieces; turn and brush with remaining apricot mixture. Broil for 4 to 6 minutes more or until chicken is tender and no longer pink. Serve immediately. If desired, serve with cooked carrots.

Nutrition Facts per serving: 221 cal., 9 g total fat (2 g sat. fat), 54 mg chol., 185 mg sodium, 19 g carbo., 16 g pro.

lemon-mustard CHICKEN

Prep: 10 minutes
Makes: 6 servings

2 to 2½ pounds meaty chicken pieces (breasts, thighs, and drumsticks)

2 tablespoons cooking oil

1 tablespoon Dijon-style mustard

1 tablespoon lemon juice

1½ teaspoons lemon-pepper seasoning

1 teaspoon dried oregano or basil, crushed

⅛ teaspoon ground red pepper

1 Skin chicken. Rinse chicken; pat dry. Place chicken pieces, bone sides up, on the unheated rack of a broiler pan. Broil 4 to 5 inches from the heat about 20 minutes or until lightly browned.

2 Meanwhile, for glaze, in a bowl stir together oil, mustard, lemon juice, lemon-pepper seasoning, oregano, and red pepper. Brush chicken with glaze. Turn chicken; brush with remaining glaze. Broil for 5 to 15 minutes more or until chicken is tender and no longer pink.

Nutrition Facts per serving: 174 cal., 10 g total fat (2 g sat. fat), 61 mg chol., 390 mg sodium, 1 g carbo., 20 g pro.

30 minutes

OR LESS

Spicy Chicken Breasts with Fruit, *recipe page 208*

italian-style CHICKEN CUTLETS

This recipe for pan-fried cutlets is quick and easy. The blend of bread crumbs, parsley, rosemary, and Parmesan creates an Italian-flavor crust around the chicken.

Prep: 15 minutes
Cook: 10 minutes
Makes: 4 servings

- **4 skinless, boneless chicken breast halves (1 to 1½ pounds total)**
- **¼ teaspoon kosher salt**
- **¼ teaspoon freshly ground black pepper**
- **¾ cup fine dry whole wheat bread crumbs**
- **2 tablespoons freshly grated Parmesan cheese**
- **1 tablespoon chopped fresh flat-leaf parsley**
- **1 teaspoon chopped fresh rosemary**
- **1 egg**
- **1 egg white**
- **2 tablespoons extra virgin olive oil**
- **Lemon wedges (optional)**

1 Place each chicken piece between two pieces of plastic wrap. Using the flat side of a meat mallet, pound chicken lightly until ½-inch thickness. Remove plastic wrap. Season chicken with kosher salt and black pepper.

2 In a shallow dish combine bread crumbs, Parmesan cheese, parsley, and rosemary. Place whole egg and egg white in another shallow dish; beat slightly. Dip chicken in beaten egg, then coat with crumb mixture.

3 In a large skillet heat olive oil over medium-high heat. Add chicken and cook for 10 to 12 minutes or until chicken is no longer pink, turning once. If desired, serve chicken with lemon wedges.

Nutrition Facts per serving: 264 cal., 11 g total fat (2 g sat. fat), 121 mg chol., 349 mg sodium, 9 g carbo., 31 g pro.

snappy CHICKEN STIR-FRY

Start to Finish: 20 minutes
Makes: 4 servings

- 1 **6-ounce package frozen pea pods**
- 1 **pound skinless, boneless chicken breast halves**
- ⅓ **cup orange juice**
- 2 **tablespoons reduced-sodium soy sauce**
- 2 **teaspoons cornstarch**
- 1 **tablespoon cooking oil**
- 2 **cups hot cooked rice**
  Chopped peanuts (optional)

1 Let pea pods stand at room temperature to partially thaw, about 20 minutes. Meanwhile, cut chicken into 1-inch pieces. In a small bowl stir together the orange juice, soy sauce, and cornstarch.*

2 Preheat a wok or large skillet over medium-high heat. Add cooking oil. Stir-fry chicken, half at a time, for 2 to 3 minutes or until no pink remains. Add more oil as necessary. Return all chicken to wok. Push chicken to the sides of the wok. Stir orange juice mixture and add to center of wok. Cook and stir until orange juice mixture is thickened and bubbly.

3 Add partially frozen pea pods to wok and stir until the whole mixture is coated with sauce. Cover and simmer the mixture for 1 minute. Serve with rice. Sprinkle with peanuts, if desired.

Nutrition Facts per serving: 310 cal., 6 g total fat (1 g sat. fat), 66 mg chol., 356 mg sodium, 30 g carbo., 30 g pro.

*Tip: If you like, omit the orange juice, reduced-sodium soy sauce, and cornstarch and instead add ½ cup desired flavor bottled stir-fry sauce.

chicken and pasta IN
PEANUT SAUCE

Makes: 4 servings

8 **ounces dried thin spaghetti**

1 **bunch baby broccoli (broccolini), cut in 2- to 3-inch lengths**

1 **medium red sweet pepper, cut in bite-size strips**

1 **pound skinless, boneless chicken breast halves**

   Salt

   Ground black pepper

1 **tablespoon olive oil**

½ **cup bottled peanut sauce**

   Crushed red pepper (optional)

1 In a Dutch oven cook pasta according to package directions; add baby broccoli and sweet pepper during last 2 minutes of cooking. Drain. Return pasta and vegetables to Dutch oven; set aside.

2 Meanwhile, halve chicken breasts horizontally. Sprinkle chicken with salt and black pepper. In 12-inch skillet cook chicken in hot oil over medium-high heat 2 minutes on each side or until no longer pink (170°F). Transfer chicken to cutting board. Slice chicken; add to pasta and vegetables. Heat through. Add peanut sauce. Pass crushed red pepper, if desired.

Nutrition Facts per serving: 467 cal., 10 g total fat (2 g sat. fat), 66 mg chol., 634 mg sodium, 55 g carbo., 37 g pro.

spring CHICKEN SCALOPPINE

Start to Finish: 30 minutes
Makes: 4 servings

4 **medium skinless, boneless chicken breast halves (1¼ to 1½ pounds)**

2 **tablespoons whole wheat flour**

¼ **teaspoon salt**

4 **tablespoons butter**

½ **cup dry white wine and/or chicken broth**

¼ **cup sliced green onions**

¼ **cup mixed snipped fresh herbs, such as oregano, thyme, lemon-thyme, and/or mint**

¼ **teaspoon coarsely ground black pepper**

⅛ **teaspoon salt**
  Steamed asparagus* (optional)

1 Place a chicken breast half between two pieces of plastic wrap. Using the flat side of a meat mallet, pound meat lightly to about ¼-inch-thick, working from the center to the edges. Remove plastic wrap. In a small bowl combine whole wheat flour and salt; sprinkle over chicken to coat and press in gently.

2 In a 12-inch skillet heat 2 tablespoons of the butter over medium heat. Cook the chicken, half at a time, for 6 to 8 minutes or until chicken is tender and no longer pink, turning once. Transfer chicken to a serving platter; cover and keep warm. Add wine and green onions to the skillet. Cook and stir for 1 to 2 minutes or until reduced to ⅓ cup, scraping up any browned bits in skillet. Remove from heat. Whisk in the remaining 2 tablespoons butter until melted. Stir in 2 tablespoons of the snipped fresh herbs, the pepper, and ⅛ teaspoon salt. (If using chicken broth, omit the ⅛ teaspoon salt.)

3 Serve chicken with steamed asparagus, if desired. Drizzle wine sauce over all. Pile remaining fresh herbs onto each serving.

Nutrition Facts per serving: 305 cal., 14 g total fat (7 g sat. fat), 114 mg chol., 384 mg sodium, 4 g carbo., 34 g pro.

*To steam asparagus spears: snap off and discard woody bases from fresh asparagus. If desired, scrape off scales. Place asparagus in a steamer basket over boiling water. Cover and steam for 4 to 6 minutes or until tender.

spicy CHICKEN BREASTS WITH FRUIT

Prep: 15 minutes
Cook: 14 minutes
Makes: 4 servings

2 teaspoons Jamaican jerk seasoning

2 fresh serrano peppers, seeded and finely chopped

4 skinless, boneless chicken breast halves

   Nonstick cooking spray

½ cup peach nectar

3 green onions, cut into 1-inch pieces

2 cups sliced, peeled peaches

1 cup sliced, pitted plums

1 tablespoon brown sugar

⅛ teaspoon salt

½ cup pitted dark sweet cherries

   Hot cooked rice (optional)

1 In a small bowl combine jerk seasoning and 1 chopped serrano pepper. Rub mixture onto both sides of chicken breasts. Lightly coat an unheated large skillet with nonstick cooking spray. Preheat skillet over medium heat. Add chicken. Cook for 8 to 10 minutes or until tender and no longer pink, turning once. Transfer to a serving platter; keep warm.

2 Add 2 tablespoons peach nectar and the onions to skillet. Cook and stir over medium heat for 4 to 5 minutes or until onions are just tender.

3 In a bowl combine remaining nectar, half of the peaches, half of the plums, remaining serrano, brown sugar, and salt. Add to skillet. Cook and stir over medium heat about 2 minutes or until slightly thickened and bubbly. Remove from heat. Stir in cherries and remaining peaches and plums. Spoon over chicken. Serve with cooked rice, if desired.

Nutrition Facts per serving: 270 cal., 2 g total fat (0 g sat. fat), 66 mg chol., 227 mg sodium, 36 g carbo., 28 g pro.

chicken breasts WITH
RASPBERRY SAUCE

Don't have seedless raspberry jam to drizzle over chicken? Then stir regular raspberry jam to soften and press through a strainer to remove seeds.

Start to Finish: 20 minutes
Makes: 4 servings

½ **teaspoon dried thyme, crushed**

½ **teaspoon dried sage, crushed**

¼ **teaspoon salt**

¼ **teaspoon pepper**

4 **skinless, boneless chicken breast halves (about 1 pound)**

Nonstick spray coating

¼ **cup seedless raspberry jam**

2 **tablespoons orange juice**

2 **tablespoons wine vinegar**

1 Combine thyme, sage, salt, and pepper; rub over chicken pieces, coating evenly.

2 Spray a 10-inch skillet with nonstick coating. Add chicken to skillet. Cook chicken over medium heat for 8 to 10 minutes or until tender and no longer pink, turning once. Remove from skillet; keep warm.

3 Stir together jam, orange juice, and vinegar; add to skillet. Boil gently, uncovered, about 2 minutes or until sauce is reduced to desired consistency. Serve chicken with sauce.

Nutrition Facts per serving: 185 cal., 4 g total fat (1 g sat. fat), 59 mg chol., 189 mg sodium, 15 g carbo., 22 g pro.

tuscany STUFFED CHICKEN BREASTS

Italian country food at its best—a tasty filling of roasted red pepper, fontina cheese, and sage.

Start to Finish: 30 minutes
Makes: 2 servings

- **2 skinless, boneless chicken breast halves (about 4 ounces each)**
- **2 ounces fontina cheese, crumbled or sliced**
- **2 roasted red sweet pepper halves or ½ cup roasted red sweet pepper halves from a jar, drained**
- **6 fresh sage leaves or ½ teaspoon dried sage, crushed**
- **2 tablespoons all-purpose flour**
- **1 tablespoon olive oil**
- **½ cup dry white wine or chicken broth**

1 Place each chicken piece, boned side up, between two pieces of clear plastic wrap. Working from the center to the edges, pound lightly with the flat side of a meat mallet to ¼-inch thickness. Remove plastic wrap. Sprinkle chicken with black pepper. Layer cheese, roasted red sweet pepper halves, and sage in the center of each breast. Fold in edges; roll up into a spiral, pressing the edges to seal. Roll in flour.

2 In an 8-inch skillet heat the oil over medium heat. Cook chicken in hot oil about 5 minutes, turning to brown all sides. Remove from skillet.

3 In the same skillet bring wine to boiling; reduce heat. Simmer, uncovered, about 2 minutes or until ¼ cup liquid remains. Return chicken to skillet. Cover and simmer for 7 to 8 minutes or until chicken is tender and no longer pink. To serve, spoon juices over chicken.

Nutrition Facts per serving: 364 cal., 19 g total fat (7 g sat. fat), 92 mg chol., 284 mg sodium, 8 g carbo., 30 g pro.

grilled CHICKEN AND VEGETABLE KABOBS

If you place the vegetables and chicken on separate skewers, you won't have to worry about the vegetables becoming overcooked before the chicken is done—just remove each skewer from the grill when it is perfectly cooked.

Prep: 20 minutes
Cook: 10 minutes
Makes: 4 servings

1 **pound skinless, boneless chicken breast halves**

4 **medium fresh mushrooms**

3 **green onions, cut into 1-inch pieces**

1 **medium red, yellow, orange, and/or green sweet pepper, cut into 1½-inch pieces**

½ **cup salsa ketchup**

2 **tablespoons jalapeño jelly**

Hot cooked rice (optional)

Thinly sliced green onion (optional)

Fresh rosemary (optional)

1 Rinse chicken; pat dry with paper towels. Cut chicken lengthwise into ½-inch-thick strips. On two long or four short skewers loosely thread chicken accordion-style. On one long or two short skewers, alternately thread the mushrooms and onions, and on one long or two short skewers, thread the sweet pepper pieces.

2 In a small saucepan heat the ketchup and jelly. Brush over chicken and vegetables.

3 Grill skewers on an uncovered grill directly over medium coals for 10 to 12 minutes or until the chicken is tender and no longer pink and the vegetables are crisp-tender, turning once and brushing with sauce. (Or preheat broiler. Place skewers on unheated rack of a broiler pan. Broil 4 to 5 inches from heat for 12 to 14 minutes, turning once and brushing with sauce.) If desired, serve over hot rice with green onion and garnish with rosemary.

Nutrition Facts per serving: 183 cal., 4 g total fat (1 g sat. fat), 59 mg chol., 314 mg sodium, 15 g carbo., 23 g pro.

lemon butter CHICKEN BREASTS

Hear the sizzle of this pan-sautéed chicken and know that dinner is just minutes away.

Start to Finish: 30 minutes
Makes: 6 servings

6   **medium boneless skinless chicken breast halves (1½ pounds)**

½   **cup all-purpose flour**

½   **teaspoon salt**

2   **teaspoons lemon pepper seasoning**

⅓   **cup butter**

2   **tablespoons lemon juice**
    Hot cooked rice or pilaf (optional)

1 Place each chicken breast half between two pieces of plastic wrap. Pound lightly into a rectangle about ¼ to ⅛ inch thick. Remove plastic wrap. In a shallow bowl, combine the flour and salt. Coat chicken breasts with flour mixture. Sprinkle chicken breasts with lemon pepper.

2 In a 12-inch skillet cook the chicken breasts in the hot butter, half at a time, over medium-high heat for about 3 minutes on each side or until brown and no longer pink. Return all of the chicken to the skillet, overlapping chicken breasts slightly. Drizzle lemon juice over the chicken breasts. Cook for 2 to 3 minutes more or until pan juices are slightly reduced. Serve chicken and pan juices over hot cooked rice or pilaf, if desired.

Nutrition Facts per serving: 258 cal., 12 g total fat (7 g sat. fat), 95 mg chol., 725 mg sodium, 8 g carb., 0 g dietary fiber, 27 g protein.

balsamic BARBECUED CHICKEN BREASTS

Make a double batch of this super-easy, all-around-tasty sauce and refrigerate the rest to try later with pork or burgers.

Prep: 15 minutes
Grill: 12 minutes
Makes: 4 servings

½ cup ketchup

¼ cup light-color corn syrup

3 tablespoons balsamic vinegar or cider vinegar

2 tablespoons thinly sliced green onions

Several dashes bottled hot pepper sauce (optional)

4 skinless, boneless chicken breast halves

1 For sauce, in a small saucepan combine ketchup, corn syrup, vinegar, green onions, and, if desired, hot pepper sauce. Bring to boiling; reduce heat. Simmer, uncovered, for 5 to 10 minutes or until desired consistency, stirring sauce occasionally.

2 For a charcoal grill, grill chicken on the rack of an uncovered grill directly over medium coals for 12 to 15 minutes or until chicken is no longer pink (170°F), turning once halfway through grilling and brushing often with sauce during the last 10 minutes of grilling. (For a gas grill, preheat grill. Reduce heat to medium. Place chicken on grill rack over heat. Cover and grill as above.)

3 To serve, reheat any remaining sauce until bubbly; serve with chicken.

Nutrition Facts per serving: 267 cal., 2 g total fat (1 g sat. fat), 82 mg chol., 432 mg sodium, 27 g carbo., 33 g pro.

pan-roasted CHICKEN WITH SHALLOTS

So simple but so delicious, this bistro-style dish is great for a special-occasion dinner.

Start to Finish: 20 minutes
Makes: 4 servings

- 8 **shallots or 1 large onion**
- 4 **medium skinless, boneless chicken breast halves (1 to 1¼ pounds total)**
- ¼ **teaspoon salt**
- ⅛ **teaspoon ground black pepper**
- 1 **tablespoon olive oil**
- 1 **medium zucchini, halved lengthwise and cut into ¼-inch slices**
- ¼ **cup snipped fresh parsley**

1 Peel shallots; halve small shallots and quarter large shallots. If using onion, cut into thin wedges (should have 1 cup shallots or onion wedges); set aside. Sprinkle chicken with salt and pepper. In a large skillet heat oil over medium-high heat. Reduce heat to medium. Add chicken; cook for 2 minutes.

2 Turn chicken. Add shallots to skillet. Cook for 8 to 10 minutes more or until chicken is no longer pink (170°F), stirring shallots frequently and turning chicken, if necessary, to brown evenly. If necessary, add additional oil to prevent sticking. Reduce heat to medium-low if chicken or shallots brown too quickly.

3 Transfer chicken and shallots to a serving platter. Cover to keep warm. Add zucchini to skillet. Cook and stir for 3 to 5 minutes or until crisp-tender. Add to platter with chicken. Sprinkle with parsley.

Nutrition Facts per serving: 193 cal., 5 g total fat (1 g sat. fat), 66 mg chol., 231 mg sodium, 9 g carbo., 28 g pro.

grilled cajun CHICKEN SANDWICHES

Start to Finish: 25 minutes
Makes: 4 servings

- 4 **skinless, boneless chicken breast halves**
  Olive oil or cooking oil
- ½ **to 1 teaspoon Cajun seasoning**
- ¼ **cup bottled Thousand Island salad dressing**
  Several dashes bottled hot pepper sauce
- 4 **hamburger buns, split and toasted**
- ½ **of a small red sweet pepper, cut into thin bite-size strips**
- ½ **cup shredded Monterey Jack cheese with jalapeño peppers (2 ounces)**
- 4 **lettuce leaves**

1 Place each chicken breast half between two pieces of plastic wrap. Pound lightly with the flat side of a meat mallet to about ½-inch thickness. Remove plastic wrap.

2 Brush both sides of chicken lightly with oil; sprinkle with Cajun seasoning. Place chicken on the rack of an uncovered grill over medium heat. Grill for 12 to 15 minutes or until no longer pink (170°F), turning once.

3 Meanwhile, stir together salad dressing and hot pepper sauce; spread over cut sides of bun bottoms. Cut chicken breasts crosswise into ½-inch slices. Layer chicken slices, sweet pepper, cheese, and lettuce on top. Add bun tops.

Nutrition Facts per serving: 429 cal., 17 g total fat (5 g sat. fat), 101 mg chol., 544 mg sodium, 26 g carbo., 40 g pro.

chicken-brown rice SALAD

When summertime comes around, it's nice to have a variety of salad recipes at hand. You can whip up this one in minutes, leaving lots of time to enjoy the great outdoors.

Start to Finish: 30 minutes
Makes: 6 servings

⅔ **cup bottled fat-free Italian salad dressing**

6 **small skinless, boneless chicken breast halves (1½ to 1¾ pounds total)**

1 **cup loose-pack frozen French-cut green beans**

3 **cups cooked brown rice or cooked kasha (roasted buckwheat groats), chilled**

1 **14-ounce can artichoke hearts, drained and quartered**

2 **cups shredded cabbage with carrot**

Lettuce leaves

① Place 3 tablespoons of the Italian salad dressing in a small bowl. Set aside remaining Italian salad dressing.

② Place chicken on the rack of an uncovered grill directly over medium coals. Grill for 12 to 15 minutes or until chicken is tender and no longer pink (170°F), turning once and brushing chicken with the 3 tablespoons dressing during the last 2 minutes.

③ Rinse green beans with cool water for 30 seconds; drain well. In a large bowl toss together beans, chilled rice, artichoke hearts, and coleslaw mix. Pour the reserved salad dressing over rice mixture; toss to gently coat.

④ Remove chicken from grill. Slice chicken. Arrange lettuce leaves on four dinner plates. Top with the rice mixture and chicken slices.

Nutrition Facts per serving: 280 cal., 3 g total fat (1 g sat. fat), 68 mg chol., 637 mg sodium, 30 g carbo., 31 g pro.

warm chicken SPINACH SALAD

This pretty main-dish salad of chicken strips, red peppers, and glossy spinach is perfect for summertime entertaining.

Start to Finish: 25 minutes
Makes: 4 servings

- 6 **cups torn spinach**
- 2 **cups torn leaf lettuce**
- 1 **medium red onion, thinly sliced**
- 2 **red or green sweet peppers, cut into bite-size strips**
- 12 **ounces skinless, boneless chicken breasts**
- ½ **teaspoon dried rosemary, crushed**
- ½ **teaspoon lemon-pepper seasoning**
- 1 **clove garlic, minced**
- 1 **tablespoon cooking oil**
- 2 **tablespoons balsamic vinegar**
- 2 **tablespoons water**
  Fresh rosemary sprigs (optional)

1 In a large salad bowl combine spinach, leaf lettuce, sliced red onion, and pepper strips. Cover and chill salad up to 2 hours.

2 Cut chicken into bite-size strips. Toss chicken with rosemary and lemon-pepper seasoning. In a wok or 10-inch skillet stir-fry chicken strips and garlic in hot oil over medium-high heat for 2 to 3 minutes or until chicken is tender and no longer pink. Remove chicken from skillet. Add to salad mixture.

3 For dressing, add vinegar and water to skillet, stirring to scrape up any browned bits. Pour dressing over salad. Toss gently to mix. Transfer to individual salad plates. Garnish with fresh rosemary, if desired.

Nutrition Facts per serving: 172 cal., 6 g total fat (1 g sat. fat), 45 mg chol., 248 mg sodium, 10 g carbo., 20 g pro.

zesty chicken WITH BLACK BEANS AND RICE

Start to Finish: 30 minutes
Makes: 4 servings

- **1 pound skinless, boneless chicken breast halves, cut into 2-inch pieces**
- **2 tablespoons cooking oil**
- **1 6- to 7.4-ounce package Spanish rice mix**
- **1¾ cups water**
- **1 15-ounce can black beans, rinsed and drained**
- **1 14.5-ounce can diced tomatoes, undrained**
- **Dairy sour cream, sliced green onions, and lime wedges (optional)**

1. In a 12-inch skillet brown the chicken pieces in 1 tablespoon of the oil over medium heat. Remove chicken from skillet.

2. Add rice mix and remaining 1 tablespoon oil to skillet; cook and stir for 2 minutes over medium heat. Stir in seasoning packet from rice mix, water, beans, and undrained tomatoes; add chicken. Bring to boiling; reduce heat. Simmer, covered, for 15 to 20 minutes or until rice is tender and chicken is no longer pink. Remove from heat and let stand, covered, for 5 minutes.

3. If desired, serve with sour cream, green onions, and lime wedges.

Nutrition Facts per serving: 424 cal., 9 g total fat (2 g sat. fat), 66 mg chol., 1,080 mg sodium, 52 g carbo., 37 g pro.

chicken FETTUCCINE

Refrigerated pasta helps make this delicious main dish quick to prepare.

Start to Finish: 25 minutes
Makes: 4 servings

- 1 **9-ounce package refrigerated fettuccine or linguine**
- ½ **cup oil-packed dried tomato strips or pieces**
- 1 **large zucchini or yellow summer squash, halved lengthwise and sliced (about 2 cups)**
- 8 **ounces skinless, boneless chicken breast halves, cut into bite-size strips**
- ½ **cup finely shredded Parmesan, Romano, or Asiago cheese (2 ounces)**
  Freshly ground black pepper
  Finely shredded Parmesan, Romano, or Asiago cheese (optional)

1 Use kitchen scissors to cut pasta in half. Cook in lightly salted boiling water according to package directions. Drain well. Return pasta to hot pan; cover and keep warm.

2 Meanwhile, drain tomato strips, reserving 2 tablespoons of the oil; set aside. In a large skillet heat 1 tablespoon of the reserved oil over medium-high heat. Add zucchini; cook and stir for 3 to 4 minutes or until crisp-tender. Remove from skillet. Reduce heat to medium. Add remaining 1 tablespoon reserved oil to skillet. Add chicken; cook and stir for 2 to 3 minutes or until no longer pink. Add zucchini, chicken, tomato strips, and the ½ cup cheese to cooked pasta; toss gently to combine. Season to taste with black pepper. If desired, sprinkle individual servings with additional cheese.

Nutrition Facts per serving: 325 cal., 8 g total fat (3 g sat. fat), 108 mg chol., 265 mg sodium, 39 g carbo., 26 g pro.

fresh corn AND CHICKEN CHOWDER

Make this soup at the height of sweet corn season—July and August—for the best and freshest flavor. If you don't want to add crushed red pepper, try a garnish of chopped fresh basil.

Start to Finish: 30 minutes
Makes: 4 servings

12 **ounces skinless, boneless chicken breast halves or chicken thighs**

4 **fresh ears of sweet corn**

1 **32-ounce container reduced-sodium chicken broth**

½ **cup green sweet pepper, chopped (1 small)**

1 **cup milk**

1¼ **cups instant mashed potato flakes**

 Salt

 Black pepper

 Crushed red pepper (optional)

1 In Dutch oven combine chicken, corn, and broth. Cover; bring to boiling over high heat. Reduce heat. Simmer 12 minutes or until chicken is no longer pink. Remove chicken and corn to cutting board.

2 Add half the sweet pepper to broth in Dutch oven. Stir in milk and potato flakes. Shred chicken using two forks. Return chicken to Dutch oven. Using a kitchen towel to hold hot corn, cut kernels from cobs. Place corn in Dutch oven; heat through. Season to taste with salt and pepper. Ladle soup into four bowls. Sprinkle each serving with remaining sweet pepper and, if desired, crushed red pepper.

Nutrition Facts per serving: 269 cal., 3 g total fat (1 g sat. fat), 54 mg chol., 721 mg sodium, 33 g carbo., 29 g pro.

chicken and asparagus
SKILLET SUPPER

Start to Finish: 20 minutes
Makes: 4 servings

- **8 skinless, boneless chicken thighs**
- **3 slices bacon, coarsely chopped**
- **½ cup chicken broth**
- **1 pound asparagus spears, trimmed**
- **1 small yellow summer squash, halved crosswise and cut in ½-inch strips**
- **2 tablespoons water**
- **4 green onions, cut in 2-inch pieces**

1 Sprinkle chicken with salt and pepper. In 12-inch skillet cook chicken and bacon over medium-high heat 12 minutes, turning to brown evenly. Carefully add broth; cover and cook 3 to 5 minutes more or until chicken is tender and no longer pink (180°F).

2 Meanwhile, in microwave-safe 2-quart dish combine asparagus, squash, and water. Sprinkle salt and pepper. Cover with vented plastic wrap. Cook on 100% power (high) 3 to 5 minutes, until vegetables are crisp-tender, stirring once. Transfer to plates. Drizzle cooking liquid; top with chicken, bacon, and onions.

Nutrition Facts per serving: 320 cal., 18 g total fat (6 g sat. fat), 134 mg chol., 626 mg sodium, 5 g carbo., 32 g pro.

watercress CHICKEN

Simmered chicken thighs in soy sauce, lime juice, ginger, and peppery watercress served over rice, makes this a delicious quick-to-fix meal.

Prep: 30 minutes
Makes: 4 servings

- 8 skinless chicken thighs (about 2½ pounds total)
- ½ teaspoon salt
- ¼ teaspoon freshly ground pepper
- 1 cup chicken broth
- 1 tablespoon soy sauce
- 1 tablespoon fresh lime juice
- 3 slices fresh ginger
- 2 large bunches (8 ounces) watercress, trimmed and cut in half
- 6 green onions, cut into 2-inch-thin strips
- ¼ cup chopped fresh cilantro
  Hot cooked rice

1 Heat 12-inch skillet over medium-high heat, 2 minutes. Sprinkle chicken with salt and pepper; add to skillet and cook 5 minutes, turning once, until lightly browned. Drain off any fat; add broth, soy sauce, lime juice, and ginger. Reduce heat and simmer chicken 20 minutes, until cooked through. With slotted spoon, transfer chicken to plate; cover and keep warm.

2 Add watercress, green onions, and cilantro to skillet; cover and cook 1 to 2 minutes, until onions are crisp-tender.

3 Divide greens and broth mixture between four serving plates. Arrange 2 thighs over top of greens, and serve with rice.

Nutrition Facts per serving with 1 cup rice: 475 cal., 9 g total fat (2.5 g sat. fat), 172 mg chol., 1,009 mg sodium, 48 g carbo., 47 g pro.

pecan-crusted CHICKEN THIGHS WITH BRAISED GREENS AND GRAPES

Start to Finish: 28 minutes
Makes: 4 servings

- **1 pound boneless, skinless chicken thighs**
- **1 egg**
- **⅓ cup finely chopped pecans**
- **⅓ cup crushed saltine or wheat crackers**
- **¼ teaspoon nutmeg**
- **1 10-ounce bag mixed salad greens**
- **4 small bunches grapes**
- **⅓ cup frozen harvest blend or white grape juice concentrate, thawed**

1 Pound chicken to slightly flatten; sprinkle salt and pepper. In shallow dish beat egg. In second dish combine pecans, crackers, and nutmeg. Dip chicken in egg then nut mixture, pressing to coat.

2 Heat 1 tablespoon olive oil in 12-inch skillet over medium heat. Cook chicken 5 to 6 minutes each side until crisp (180°F). Remove; cover. In hot skillet cook and stir greens until beginning to wilt. Remove; sprinkle salt and pepper.

3 Heat 1 teaspoon olive oil in 10-inch skillet. Cook grapes 3 to 4 minutes until skins begin to burst. Add juice concentrate; cook 1 minute more. To serve, drizzle juices over chicken and greens.

Nutrition Facts per serving: 367 cal., 18 g total fat (3 g sat. fat), 147 mg chol., 485 mg sodium, 27 g carbo., 27 g pro.

chicken caesar BURGERS

Chicken Caesar salad has become a restaurant favorite over the years, so it figures the flavors would taste great tucked into grilled ground chicken patties.

Prep: 15 minutes
Grill: 6 minutes
Makes: 4 servings

1 **egg**

1 **pound ground chicken**

1 **cup fresh bread crumbs
    (2 slices)**

¼ **cup grated Parmesan cheese**

2 **teaspoons anchovy paste**

1 **teaspoon lemon juice**

1 **teaspoon Worcestershire
    sauce**

1 **clove garlic, finely chopped**

¼ **teaspoon black pepper**

½ **cup sour cream**

½ **cup bottled Caesar salad
    dressing**

4 **pitas (6 inch), split open one-
    third of the way around**

Tomato slices (optional)

Shredded romaine lettuce

❶ Heat gas grill to medium-hot or prepare charcoal grill with medium-hot coals.

❷ Beat egg in large bowl. Mix in chicken, bread crumbs, Parmesan cheese, anchovy paste, lemon juice, Worcestershire sauce, garlic, and pepper.

❸ Between sheets of waxed paper coated with nonstick cooking spray, flatten rounded ½ cup mixture to 5-inch patty, making four burgers.

❹ Grill burgers for 6 to 8 minutes or until instant-read meat thermometer inserted in center of burger registers 165°F; turning once.

❺ In small bowl combine sour cream and dressing. In each pita, place a burger and, if desired, a tomato slice. Top each tomato slice with some of the sour cream mixture and lettuce.

Nutrition Facts per burger: 538 cal., 28 g total fat (7 g sat. fat), 167 mg chol., 1,328 mg sodium, 36 g carbo., 34 g pro.

tex-mex CHICKEN TOSTADAS

Ground chicken makes quick work of this open-face Tex-Mex sandwich.

Start to Finish: 25 minutes
Makes: 4 servings

- **4 8-inch flour tortillas**
- **1 pound ground raw chicken**
- **1 teaspoon chili powder**
- **1 8-ounce bottle medium or hot salsa**
- **1 15-ounce can black beans or pinto beans**
- **2 tablespoons diced pimiento**
- **1 cup chopped lettuce**
- **¼ cup thinly sliced radishes**
- **¼ cup shredded cheddar cheese (1 ounce)**
- **1 2.25-ounce can sliced pitted ripe olives**
- **Dairy sour cream (optional)**
- **2 tablespoons thinly sliced green onion**
- **Avocado slices (optional)**

1 For tostada shells, place tortillas in a single layer directly on the middle oven rack. Bake in a 350°F oven about 6 minutes, turning halfway through baking time, or until golden and crisp. (If tortillas bubble during baking, puncture the bubble with a fork.) Set aside and cover to keep warm.

2 Meanwhile, in a 10-inch skillet cook and stir chicken and chili powder over medium heat for 5 to 7 minutes or until chicken is cooked through. Stir in salsa. Set aside; keep warm.

3 Drain beans, reserving liquid. In a small saucepan stir beans over low heat until heated through. With a potato masher or fork, mash beans adding enough reserved bean liquid to make spreadable consistency. Heat through.

4 To assemble, place a warm tortilla on each dinner plate. Spread with a thin layer of beans. Top beans with some of the chicken mixture, pimiento, lettuce, radishes, cheese, olives, sour cream (if desired), and green onion. Garnish with avocado, if desired.

Nutrition Facts per serving: 365 cal., 15 g total fat (4 g sat. fat), 62 mg chol., 809 mg sodium, 38 g carbo., 29 g pro.

soft-shell CHICKEN TACOS

Start to Finish: 20 minutes
Makes: 4 soft-shell tacos

1　2¼- to 2½-pound purchased roasted chicken

4　7- to 8-inch flour tortillas

½　cup dairy sour cream salsa or Mexican-flavor dip

1　large red, green, or yellow sweet pepper, cut into bite-size strips

1½　cups shredded lettuce

1 Remove skin and bones from chicken and discard. Coarsely shred 2 cups of the chicken. Reserve remaining chicken for another use.

2 Lightly spread one side of each tortilla with dip. Top with chicken, sweet pepper, and lettuce. Top with the remaining dip. Fold tortillas in halves to serve.

Nutrition Facts per serving: 284 cal., 13 g total fat (5 g sat. fat), 82 mg chol., 479 mg sodium, 19 g carbo., 23 g pro.

metric information

The charts on this page provide a guide for converting measurements from the U.S. customary system, which is used throughout this book, to the metric system.

PRODUCT DIFFERENCES

Most of the ingredients called for in the recipes in this book are available in most countries. However, some are known by different names. Here are some common American ingredients and their possible counterparts:

- Sugar (white) is granulated, fine granulated, or castor sugar.
- Powdered sugar is icing sugar.
- All-purpose flour is enriched, bleached, or unbleached white household flour. When self-rising flour is used in place of all-purpose flour in a recipe that calls for leavening, omit the leavening agent (baking soda or baking powder) and salt.
- Light-color corn syrup is golden syrup.
- Cornstarch is cornflour.
- Baking soda is bicarbonate of soda.
- Vanilla or vanilla extract is vanilla essence.
- Green, red, or yellow sweet peppers are capsicums or bell peppers.
- Golden raisins are sultanas.

VOLUME AND WEIGHT

The United States traditionally uses cup measures for liquid and solid ingredients. The chart, top right, shows the approximate imperial and metric equivalents. If you are accustomed to weighing solid ingredients, the following approximate equivalents will be helpful.

- 1 cup butter, castor sugar, or rice = 8 ounces = $\frac{1}{2}$ pound = 250 grams
- 1 cup flour = 4 ounces = $\frac{1}{4}$ pound = 125 grams
- 1 cup icing sugar = 5 ounces = 150 grams

Canadian and U.S. volume for a cup measure is 8 fluid ounces (237 ml), but the standard metric equivalent is 250 ml.

1 British imperial cup is 10 fluid ounces.

In Australia, 1 tablespoon equals 20 ml, and there are 4 teaspoons in the Australian tablespoon.

Spoon measures are used for smaller amounts of ingredients. Although the size of the tablespoon varies slightly in different countries, for practical purposes and for recipes in this book, a straight substitution is all that's necessary. Measurements made using cups or spoons always should be level unless stated otherwise.

COMMON WEIGHT RANGE REPLACEMENTS

Imperial / U.S.	Metric
$\frac{1}{2}$ ounce	15 g
1 ounce	25 g or 30 g
4 ounces ($\frac{1}{4}$ pound)	115 g or 125 g
8 ounces ($\frac{1}{2}$ pound)	225 g or 250 g
16 ounces (1 pound)	450 g or 500 g
1$\frac{1}{4}$ pounds	625 g
1$\frac{1}{2}$ pounds	750 g
2 pounds or 2$\frac{1}{4}$ pounds	1,000 g or 1 Kg

OVEN TEMPERATURE EQUIVALENTS

Fahrenheit Setting	Celsius Setting*	Gas Setting
300°F	150°C	Gas Mark 2 (very low)
325°F	160°C	Gas Mark 3 (low)
350°F	180°C	Gas Mark 4 (moderate)
375°F	190°C	Gas Mark 5 (moderate)
400°F	200°C	Gas Mark 6 (hot)
425°F	220°C	Gas Mark 7 (hot)
450°F	230°C	Gas Mark 8 (very hot)
475°F	240°C	Gas Mark 9 (very hot)
500°F	260°C	Gas Mark 10 (extremely hot)
Broil	Broil	Grill

*Electric and gas ovens may be calibrated using celsius. However, for an electric oven, increase celsius setting 10 to 20 degrees when cooking above 160°C. For convection or forced air ovens (gas or electric) lower the temperature setting 25°F/10°C when cooking at all heat levels.

BAKING PAN SIZES

Imperial / U.S.	Metric
9×1$\frac{1}{2}$-inch round cake pan	22- or 23×4-cm (1.5 L)
9×1$\frac{1}{2}$-inch pie plate	22- or 23×4-cm (1 L)
8×8×2-inch square cake pan	20×5-cm (2 L)
9×9×2-inch square cake pan	22- or 23×4.5-cm (2.5 L)
11×7×1$\frac{1}{2}$-inch baking pan	28×17×4-cm (2 L)
2-quart rectangular baking pan	30×19×4.5-cm (3 L)
13×9×2-inch baking pan	34×22×4.5-cm (3.5 L)
15×10×1-inch jelly roll pan	40×25×2-cm
9×5×3-inch loaf pan	23×13×8-cm (2 L)
2-quart casserole	2 L

U.S. / STANDARD METRIC EQUIVALENTS

$\frac{1}{8}$ teaspoon = 0.5 ml	$\frac{1}{3}$ cup = 3 fluid ounces = 75 ml
$\frac{1}{4}$ teaspoon = 1 ml	$\frac{1}{2}$ cup = 4 fluid ounces = 125 ml
$\frac{1}{2}$ teaspoon = 2 ml	$\frac{1}{3}$ cup = 5 fluid ounces = 150 ml
1 teaspoon = 5 ml	$\frac{3}{4}$ cup = 6 fluid ounces = 175 ml
1 tablespoon = 15 ml	1 cup = 8 fluid ounces = 250 ml
2 tablespoons = 25 ml	2 cups = 1 pint = 500 ml
$\frac{1}{4}$ cup = 2 fluid ounces = 50 ml	1 quart = 1 litre

index

Note: Page references in *italics* refer to photographs.

235